FV

 St. Louis Community College

Forest Park
Florissant Valley
Meramec

Instructional Resources
St. Louis, Missouri

GAYLORD

RACE, MYTH and the NEWS

For Sheri,
and for Mom and Dad

RACE, MYTH and the NEWS

Christopher P. Campbell

SAGE Publications
International Educational and Professional Publisher
Thousand Oaks   London   New Delhi

For information address:

SAGE Publications, Inc.
2455 Teller Road
Thousand Oaks, California 91320

SAGE Publications Ltd.
6 Bonhill Street
London EC2A 4PU
United Kingdom

SAGE Publications India Pvt. Ltd.
M-32 Market
Greater Kailash I
New Delhi 110 048 India

Printed in the United States of America

Library of Congress Cataloging-in-Publication Data

Campbell, Christopher P.
   Race, myth and the news / Christopher P. Campbell
      p. cm.
   Includes bibliographical references and index.
   ISBN 0-8039-5871-4 (cloth: alk. paper). — ISBN 0-8039-5872-2
   (pbk.: alk. paper)
   1. Racism in the press—United States. 2. Mass media and race
relations—United States. 3. Television broadcasting of news—
Political aspects—United States. 4. Television broadcasting of
news—Social aspects—United States. I. Title.
PN4888.R3C36   1995
305.8—dc20   94-49397

This book is printed on acid-free paper.

95 96 97 98 99 10 9 8 7 6 5 4 3 2 1

Sage Production Editor: Astrid Virding
Ventura Typesetter and Design: Joe Cribben

Contents

Acknowledgments

The primary research for this study was supported by a grant from the National Endowment for the Humanities for faculty members from Historically Black Colleges and Universities. The final stages of the study were supported by a grant from the Humanities Endowment Committee at Xavier University of Louisiana.

I also owe thanks to the following:

Dr. Mazharul Haque and Dr. Art Kaul of the University of Southern Mississippi for the ideas, encouragement and support that they provided during the various stages of my research.

My brother, Dr. Richard Campbell, who was also a source of encouragement and whose research inspired the direction of my own.

Dr. Yasue Kuwahara of Northern Kentucky University, to whom I have often turned for support and whose critique was essential in completing the final draft of this book.

My students—especially those from Soldan High School in St. Louis, where I taught from 1977 to 1981, and from Xavier University of Louisiana, where I teach now. It was their "readings" of the news that was the initial source of inspiration for this study.

Sage Publications, especially my editors, Sophy Craze and Myrna Reagons; and to Kris Bergstad (copyeditor) and Astrid Virding (production editor).

My colleagues at Xavier University, especially Dr. Anne Barron and the late Sr. Rosemarie Kleinhaus.

The family members, friends and colleagues who so diligently videotaped the local news in or near their hometowns for the purposes of this study. They include Patti and Rick Wade (Atlanta); Milly and Kenny Sharfe (Billings); Margo and Al Stearns (Cheyenne); Trish and Greg Gerber (Chicago); Yasue Kuwahara (Cincinnati); Nancy and Harry Campbell (Columbus); Molly and Dick Campbell (Dayton); Dianna and Dick Campbell (Detroit); Jackie and Jim Shaw (Fargo); Karen Johnson and Kelly Herold (Hattiesburg); Dana Stearns (Houston); Sebreana Domingue (Lafayette); Greg Picard (Los Angeles); Eileen Gleeson and James Fischer (Milwaukee); Charlene and Mike Sethney (Minneapolis); Robin and Dave Kent (Nashville); Holly and Drew Perkins (New York); Karen Fischer (Norfolk); Betty and Bob Jondahl (Phoenix); David Fischer (Portland); Pam and Michael Fournier (St. Louis); Mike Killenberg (St. Petersburg); Diane Picard (Salinas); Nona Watkins (Salt Lake); Susan Friedewald and Roger Jones (San Francisco); Judy and Gene Otto (Seattle); and Annie and Tom Campbell (Syracuse).

My wife, Dr. Sheri Hoem, whose constant support enabled me to get through this project.

CHAPTER 1

Introduction

On January 19, 1993, nearly 9 months after South Central Los Angeles erupted in the wake of the Rodney King verdict, the 6 p.m. broadcast of the local KNBC-TV news carried a 30-second story about the Los Angeles Police Commission's approval of a $1 million plan to "better defend the city against rioting." As anchor Jess Marlow introduced the story, an illustration over his shoulder read "RIOT READINESS" and showed a helmeted police officer armed with a machine gun. Marlow told the audience, "The first hurdle to better equip the Los Angeles Police Department in the event of another riot was cleared today in downtown Los Angeles." As viewers saw several shots of the commission's meeting in progress, Marlow explained, "The police commission approved a request for more than a million dollars to be spent on new equipment. The department says it needs more riot gear—including tear gas and ammunition—to better defend the city against rioting." The story ended with a close-up shot of police commander Scott LaChasse, who told KNBC, "The message is that we're ready and willing to protect the city. We need the proper equipment and other logistical items to do so."

The KNBC journalists who prepared the report did not question the police commander's commonsense explanation of the commission's decision. The police needed a million dollars to protect the city against citizen uprisings. Marlow's acquiescent telling of the story, and the eerie "RIOT READINESS" graphic of a helmeted, machine gun-toting police officer, mirrored that common sense. The need to "better equip the Los Angeles Police Department in the event of another riot" was implicit, as was the commission's approval of a million dollar expenditure on "more riot gear to better defend the city against rioting."

For KNBC's journalists and for many of the station's viewers, the story was likely one that simply reflected the needs of a city capable of erupting again. It simply made *sense* to prepare for such an eruption. Cultural critic Stuart Hall (1980) would describe this understanding of the story as its "preferred" reading. He explains,

> The domains of "preferred meanings" have the whole social order embedded in them as a set of meanings, practices and beliefs: the everyday knowledge of social structures, of "how things work for all practical purposes in this culture," the rank order of power and interest and the structure of legitimations, limits sanctions. (p. 134)

But not all of the audience members accepted the "riot readiness" narrative's common sense. For instance, Susan Anderson, a Los Angeles-based writer and community activist, had a very different reaction to the commission's decision:

> We live in a city that sees fit to come up with a million dollars, I don't know from where, for their . . . shopping list of riot gear so that . . . we can prepare for war. But our city doesn't seem to be able to come up with the resources to deal with the hungry people that are here, the people that don't have work. (quoted in Mannes, 1993)

Anderson had a similar reaction to local television coverage of other Los Angeles police preparations for a possible repeat of the uprising:

> When I saw the police doing their riot training out by Dodger Stadium, I knew that there would be people, when they see these pictures and hear what they're doing, who would feel reassured.

. . . I was very distressed. I hated to think of the confrontations that might occur if something breaks out again. (quoted in Mannes, 1993)

Anderson's interpretation of the events contrasts with the understanding implied by KNBC's journalists. Hall describes readings that question the "preferred" meanings as "negotiated" or "oppositional" readings. A negotiated reading "accords the privileged position to the dominant definitions of events while reserving the right to make a more negotiated application" (Hall, 1980, p. 137). An oppositional reading "detotalizes the message in the preferred code in order to retotalize the message within some alternative framework of reference" (p. 138). Anderson's negotiated/oppositional reading questions the commonsense notions that are embedded in coverage that reflects the news profession's dominant culture perception of daily events. The purpose of this book is to examine how majority culture perceptions ("preferred readings") reflected in local television news coverage feed mythological notions about Americans of color—notions that can contribute to contemporary racist attitudes. Like Anderson's reading of the news, which is contrary to the sense-making intent of local TV journalists, my study reads the news not only for the broadcasters' manifest intentions but also in terms of the connotative messages the stories impart about life outside of mainstream, white America. It examines the possibility that local television news coverage—grounded in traditions, values and routines that dictate a kind of tunnel vision—sustains a contemporary racist mythology that advances erroneous notions about Americans of color.

Spring 1993 marked the 25th anniversary of the publication of the Kerner Commission (1968) report—a study commissioned by President Lyndon Johnson to examine the violent unrest that gripped urban America in the late 1960s. That study found America to be "moving toward two societies, one black, one white—separate and unequal" (p. 1). The Kerner Commission— made up of city, state and national politicians, the executive director of the NAACP, the president of the AFL-CIO, the CEO of Litton Industries and the police chief of Atlanta—attempted to determine what had happened, why it had happened and what could be done to ease the unrest and improve the quality of life in America's impoverished inner cities. Included in the study was an analysis of the role of the news media and its portrayal of black America. Wrote the commission,

> Along with the country as a whole, the press has too long basked in a white world, looking out of it, if at all, with white men's eyes and a white perspective. That is no longer good enough. The painful process of readjustment that is required of the American news media must begin now. They must make a reality of integration—in both their product and personnel. They must insist on the highest standards of accuracy—not only reporting single events with care and skepticism, but placing each event into meaningful perspective. They must report the travail of our cities with compassion and depth. (p. 389)

The commission conducted numerous field surveys and interviews and arranged for a quantitative analysis of news coverage before, during and after the riots. Its findings painted a bleak picture of the work of the virtually all-white journalism profession, and the commission issued a number of recommendations to improve the situation. It called for news organizations to make aggressive efforts to increase the number of African Americans in all levels of their ranks and to discontinue their practice of ignoring the black community in their news coverage.

Should President Bill Clinton commission a similar study to examine the reasons for the violence that broke out in Los Angeles, it is likely that a new look at the news media would produce findings and recommendations remarkably similar to the Kerner Commission's. Although there was a modest increase in the number of minority journalists during the 1970s, the commission's recommendations have gone largely unheeded. Roughly half of the daily newspapers in the United States employ *no* journalists of color. Ninety-five percent of all newspaper journalists are white, and the statistics in broadcast news are only slightly better. The gains in hiring made in the 1970s were lost during the 1980s. And though news coverage of African American life may have increased, it still often suffers from the lack of perspective described by the commission.

Americans who rely on mainstream journalism and prime-time television for their perception of race relations were likely taken aback by the rebellion in Los Angeles. The popular media in this country have advanced a myth of racial tolerance and assimilation that fails to explain the violent reaction to the Rodney King verdict. Prime-time fictional TV (and not just *The Cosby Show*) shows us that The American Dream is within the reach of any hardworking citizen; the news—often reported by financially and socially successful minority journalists—frequently implies that those who fail to attain financial and social success have only themselves to blame. Mass media acknowledgment of the realities of racism is almost exclusively limited to rap music or to films by African-American filmmakers.

The Kerner Commission's report, as well as many of the studies of race and the news that followed over the next quarter-century, relied primarily on quantitative data. Those studies tell us how many minority journalists are working in the media, how many have left their jobs, how many stories have been written about minority communities, how many have reflected stereotypes, and so on. Although many of these studies are useful in explaining the problem of racism in the news media, they tend to leave just as much unexplained. What myths about race are being reflected in the news? How do those myths stand up against the realities of racism? How do the values, ideology and traditions of journalism contribute to the myths? Does the very nature of news as a purveyor of "common sense" diminish the ability of journalists to portray society in a representative manner that offers true perspective? Why is it that well-intentioned journalists—of all colors—advance the racial myths that so many white Americans cling to? How are public perceptions affected by those myths? How do the attitudes identified in research on contemporary racism—including *modern, aversive, everyday* and *enlightened* racism, as well as the *assimilationist* mythology of prime-time television—surface in the news?

The answers to these questions cannot be easily found in quantifying the responses of journalists to survey questions nor in the statistics generated by detailed content analyses. A more appropriate means of getting at the root of these myths seems to be through qualitative approaches to the research, and this study relies on the interpretive approach. Interpretive research allows for a reading of media "texts" in the context of larger cultural meanings. As Seiter (1987) writes, "When we watch something like the news, we tend not to think of the active production of signs involved in TV, but receive the news rather as pure information" (p. 23). The small body of interpretive research that has examined race and the media has provided important and useful insight into contemporary American racism. It is the intention of this study to add to that body of research.

Examining the meaning-making capacity of local television news seems a worthwhile endeavor, especially considering American reliance on the broadcasts for information about the events of the day. The Roper Organization (1993) tells us that most Americans continue to turn to television instead of newspapers for their news, that they find television news more credible than newspapers, and that they believe television journalists perform their duties more ably. Earlier Roper studies (1982) found that 70% of Americans believe that local television journalists perform their job in an excellent fashion, a higher ranking than newspaper journalists, police officers, politicians, school officials or members of the clergy. Given the kind of public trust that local TV journalists maintain, the stories, images and words they air each night seem worthy of the textual analyses that comprise this study.

In investigating local television journalism's contribution to America's racial mythology, I have analyzed a considerable sampling of local television news as "text." That is, by closely "reading" news programming from a spectrum of American cities, I have attempted to interpret the news in terms of its symbolic and cultural meanings about race. These analyses draw on other critical and cultural studies of news and race, utilizing a combination of ideological and semiotic approaches.

The newscasts viewed for this study were videotaped by family members, friends and colleagues across the country to represent a variety of geographical locations, ethnic populations and market sizes (see Appendix A for a listing of the TV markets included). I gathered videotapes of 39 hours of local television newscasts from 29 cities around the country that aired on January 18, 19, and 20, 1993. This sampling was intended to offer a representative look at what Americans saw on their local evening newscasts in January 1993. The tapes include coverage of events surrounding the national Martin Luther King, Jr. holiday, which was celebrated on January 18.

The second chapter of this book attempts to put this study in context; that is, it tries to provide a proper theoretical framework for an interpretive analysis of race and the news. It looks at related research and includes an examination of the nature of news in terms of its "meaning-making" role in American culture. It also identifies the key concepts that are addressed in the book, including "common sense" and "myth," as well as explanations of the different types of racism that will be explored.

The third chapter examines lingering vestiges of traditional racism—the sort of overt racism that many Americans consider a thing of the past—in local television news coverage. The chapter discusses the underrepresentation of minorities in the news and how that "invisibility" contributes to a "myth of marginality" about nonwhite Americans. It argues that the general lack of coverage of minority issues and minority communities contributes to a sense of "otherness" about Americans of color. The chapter also argues that coverage that overlooks the complexities of existence in minority communities while unwaveringly doting on white life and majority culture reflects a common sense about minority life that places nonwhites in the margins, outside of mainstream American society. The chapter includes analyses of three stories that reflect minority marginalization and the persistence of overt racism in the news. It points out that only a few of the hundreds of stories reviewed for this study reflected the blatant racial insensitivity that is associated with the traditional racism of the past. But it argues that even infrequent episodes of this kind of insensitivity—when compounded by the news media's general underrepresentation of minority life—can contribute to a dangerous ignorance about people of color and a continuance of discrimination and injustice.

The fourth chapter examines the persistence of racial stereotyping in local television news coverage in the 1990s. The chapter argues that a "myth of difference" is subtly (and probably inadvertently) reflected in coverage that defines black success in terms of sports and entertainment while emphasizing minority criminal activity. The chapter analyzes several stories that reflect predetermined notions about minorities and minority communities. It argues that the nature of the news-gathering process often dictates simplistic explanations of events that can perpetuate traditional myths about race. The chapter also examines a Virginia station's coverage of a shooting that—by eschewing the typical police account and focusing on the victim and his family—does not feed the standard mythology.

The fifth chapter applies the findings of researchers who have examined prime-time fictional television to the nonfictional images of local television news. The chapter analyzes coverage of the Martin Luther King, Jr. holiday. It argues that the coverage reflects "a myth of assimilation" about race relations in the United States and contributes to an "enlightened" form of racism; that is, the coverage assigned American racism to images of the past, bolstering the attitudes of white Americans who point to the success of a few prominent minority figures as an indication that racism no longer exists in the United States. The chapter discusses television's understanding of socioeconomic classes and how that understanding further contributes to the attitudes of contemporary racism. It also examines how coverage of King Day by both white and black journalists contributed to assimilationist mythology. The chapter ends with a discussion of coverage of King Day by a station in Billings, MT, a station that—remarkably—avoided the "commonsense" mythology of racial harmony and evoked a much less optimistic (and possibly more realistic) understanding of race relations in America.

The sixth chapter compares newspaper coverage of the Martin Luther King, Jr. holiday with the coverage that was seen on local television news. It attempts to determine if the kinds of myths reflected in local TV journalism also surface in the newspaper. That discussion argues that mythological notions about race extend across all types of news media. But it also points out that the newspaper medium's potential to include longer and more analytical stories gives it the capability to contradict standard racial mythology.

The final chapter summarizes my findings and also raises the possibility that nonnews media are providing Americans with more accurate portraits of race in America. Popular media—in the form of TV talk shows, call-in radio shows, Spike Lee films, MTV and rap music—now contribute to America's political and social dialogue. The final chapter argues that the "New News" may be having a more profound impact on the discussion of race in America than conventional news programming. This study does not intend to provide a solution to the existence of racism in contemporary American journalism. As Tuchman (1978) suggests, that would require "news professionals to question the very premises of the news net and their own routine practices" (p. 215). What it does intend to do is raise questions about those news practices and about contemporary racism by interpreting the symbolic nature of news "texts." Certainly, the vast majority of contemporary American journalists would consider their work to be free of imagery that could contribute to racist attitudes. But the attitudes of contemporary racism can be subtle, and the news production process—which is ultimately affected by factors including individual socialization, newsroom values and the intensity of deadline pressure— hardly allows for careful consideration of the complex myth-making capacity of the news. Local TV news programs rely on rapid-fire stories replete with dramatic visuals, making them especially proficient at reinforcing America's racial mythology.

Twenty-five years ago, the Kerner Commission determined that the news media—dominated by white journalists and majority culture ideology—had advanced attitudes that fostered racial discrimination and prejudice and contributed to the conditions that led to violent unrest in America's urban centers. This study argues that journalists are similarly advancing the attitudes of contemporary racism. Though the attitudes may not be as overt as those of the past, they would appear to be equally dangerous; the great majority of people of color remain impoverished, living at the social and financial periphery of American life. As cultural critic Cornel West (1993) argues,

> We must acknowledge that as a people—E Pluribus Unum—we are on a slippery slope toward economic strife, social turmoil, and cultural chaos. If we go down, we go down together. The Los Angeles upheaval forced us to see not only that we are not connected in ways we would like to be but also, in a more profound sense, that this failure to connect binds us even more tightly together. The paradox of race in America is that our common destiny is more pronounced and imperiled precisely when our divisions are deeper.

The Civil War and its legacy speak loudly here. And our divisions
are growing deeper. (p. 4)

Even though many changes have occurred in society and in
the media industry since the Kerner report, life for many ethnic
minorities in America remains hopeless, powerless. For news
coverage to perform its duty properly as the watchdog of American democracy, that coverage would need to put in perspective
the complex historical and social issues that affect racial attitudes. Without that perspective, we cannot expect the news
media to have much effect on the status of race relations in
the 1990s.

CHAPTER 2

Common Sense,
Myth, News and Racism

The starting point of these reflections was usually a feeling of impatience at the sight of the "naturalness" with which newspapers, art and common sense constantly dress up a reality which, even though it is the one we live in, is undoubtedly determined by history. . . . I hate seeing Nature and History confused at every turn, and I wanted to track down, in the decorative display of *what-goes-without-saying*, the ideological abuse which, in my view, is hidden there.

—*Roland Barthes (1957/1972, p. 11)*

In short, given the given, not everything else follows. Common sense is not what the mind cleared of cant spontaneously apprehends; it is what the mind filled with presuppositions . . . concludes.

—*Clifford Geertz (1983, p. 84)*

When . . . racism is transmitted in routine practices that seem "normal," at least for the dominant group, this can only mean that racism is often not recognized, not acknowledged—let alone problematized—by the dominant group.

—*Philomena Essed (1991, p. 10)*

It is an oft-repeated anecdote: When asked for his definition of news, network journalist David Brinkley is said to have responded, "News is what I say it is." His terse reply could be taken as a pompous reflection of news media elitism. But it also could be taken as an insightful description of the way in which journalists do their work. News values, newsroom social forces, journalism education, deadline pressure and any number of other factors contribute to a process that works without introspection, without definition. The result is news that reflects the journalistic "common sense" that is evident in Brinkley's definition and in the day-to-day workings of the news media. But analyses of the journalistic process and of the concept of common sense, itself, indicate the significant consequences of news media that, by routine, serve up a common-sense view of the world that may not be so *common*—especially in terms of its representation of American pluralism—nor entirely *sensible*—especially in terms of its lack of history, of perspective.

It is more likely that the news that results from the journalistic routine is carrying interpretations not considered by the journalists, themselves—interpretations that carry considerable mythical weight. These myths impose cultural understandings that feed a hegemonic consensus about American society. Considering the multicultural makeup of that society, the most dangerous (and the most common) myths may be those that reflect white, middle- and upper-class notions of society and impede multicultural understanding and interpretation. In Barthes's (1957/1972) terms, these myths reveal a dangerous *naturalness* (or *common sense*) about contemporary racism while denying its *history* and failing to place it in perspective.

The nature of local television news makes it especially susceptible to myth-making. Stories are brief—many less than half a minute—and feature quick sound bites accompanied by rapid fire video. The stories deemed worthy of coverage are those that can best be told with pictures: fires, news conferences, crime scenes and handcuffed criminal suspects dominate the newscasts. The brevity of the stories calls for the most simple explanations of events, ignoring the complexities that tend to surround many

12

stories. And the bulky process of local TV news hardly allows for much thoughtful analysis of the day's events. Photographers, reporters, videotape editors, producers and anchors—usually under remarkable pressure to meet the evening's deadlines—can each dramatically affect the way a story is told.

A number of research approaches have been utilized in moving toward a cultural understanding of mass media and myth. Cultural anthropology, sociology, linguistics, psychology, psychoanalysis, literary criticism and many cross-disciplinary approaches have been used in attempting to interpret the deeper meanings that lay just beneath the surface of a culture's artifacts. Much of the research in this area indicates the need to, in James Carey's (1989) words, "interpret the interpretations" (p. 60). Indirectly, the research also reflects a likelihood that contemporary racism in America is being fostered by the news media's "commonsense" myths despite even the best intentions of journalists caught up in a system dominated by majority culture values and sensibilities.

Although this study specifically analyzes local television news, its theoretical framework is rooted in more general studies of mass media and journalism. It applies the thinking of critical and cultural studies scholars to the issue of media racism. The purposes of this chapter are to (a) provide theoretical support for an interpretive study of race and news, (b) describe the nature of news in terms of cultural *meaning making,* especially as *myth* and as *common sense,* and (c) summarize research on contemporary racism and on race and the mass media.

The approach to this study reflects my agreement with the qualitative/interpretive researchers who view communication as a "symbolic action." As Pauly (1991) writes, "In brief: qualitative studies investigate meaning-making" (p. 2). Theoretical approaches to research set interpretive research apart from traditional, quantitative mass communication approaches. As Carey (1989) explains,

> A cultural science of communication . . . views human behavior—or, more accurately, human action—as a text. Our task is to construct a "reading" of the text. The text itself is a sequence of symbols—speech, writing, gesture—that contain interpretations. Our task, like that of a literary critic, is to interpret the interpretations. (p. 60)

It is the aim of this study to interpret local television news in a "holistic" fashion. Though my primary focus will be on interpreting the symbols of local television news, I will also consider audience reactions and the potential effects of the messages; that is, my interpretations will consider the implications of those messages within a larger cultural system. This approach seems the most suited to get at some understanding of how the news makes meanings about race in America.

▨ News, Myth and Common Sense

The qualitative approach to the study of news has been valuable in providing cultural and critical analyses of the process of news, raising questions about journalism's traditional conventions and trappings, much of it in terms of news mythology. Because much of this study will refer to the concept of the *myth*, I should clarify my use of the term. As Abrams (1988) explains, "A reader should be alert to the bewildering variety of applications of the term 'myth' in contemporary criticism" (p. 123). I use *myth* not in the grand storytelling tradition associated with ancient cultures, but in the sense of the stories that modern societies unwittingly create to reduce life's contradictions and complexities. Lévi-Strauss (1967), Barthes (1957/1972), Fiske and Hartley (1978) and others have analyzed myths in semiotic terms, interpreting *cultural myths* as meaning-making systems that help explain societal attitudes, behaviors and ideologies. It is in this sense that I approach myth, though I should also point out that I feel this approach does not exclude the common, pejorative use of the term. For instance, when speaking of "news myths" or "racial myths," the negative connotation seems appropriate even though it does not embody the complexity of the cultural myth approach.

I also believe that this approach does not necessarily contradict traditional understanding of mythologies. So even though mythologist Joseph Campbell may have bemoaned the lack of powerful myths in the modern world, some of the functions of traditional mythology persist in today's cultural myths. For example, Campbell (1988) contends that the traditional myths "support . . . and validate a certain social order" (p. 31), and reflect truths in "bounded communities" (p. 22). He offers this example:

> The ten commandments say, "Thou shalt not kill." Then the next chapter says, "Go into Canaan and kill everybody in it." That is a bounded field. The myths of participation and love pertain only to the in-group, and the out-group is totally other. (p. 22)

Contemporary mythology, especially about race and class, would appear to contribute to a similar social order that dictates who participates and who doesn't. My approach to the modern cultural myth, then, does not completely preclude other understandings of the term, but views myth in all its connotations as a society's powerful system of belief, a system that may not accurately reflect all of that society's constituencies.

This study draws on the work of researchers who have addressed the myth-making capacity of the news media. Bird and Dardenne (1988) describe news myths in terms of "continuing stories" with themes that are "rearticulated and reinterpreted over time, themes that are derived from culture and that feed back into it" (p. 72). They explain,

> News . . . is a way in which people create order out of disorder, transforming knowing into telling. News offers more than fact— it offers reassurance and familiarity in shared community experiences; it provides credible answers to baffling questions, and ready explanations of complex phenomena such as unemployment and inflation. (p. 70)

Similarly, Fiske and Hartley (1978) describe news myths as the symbolic, "cultural meanings" (p. 42) that go beyond the literal, connotative meanings of news stories. In their analysis of a news story televised in England about British troop reinforcements in Northern Ireland, they explain how a soldier included in the story carries with him a great deal of cultural symbolism:

> The image in our film of a soldier clipping a magazine on to his rifle as he peers from his sandbagged bunker fortress in Belfast

can activate the myth by which we currently "understand" the
army. This myth . . . is that the army consists of ordinary men,
doing a professional and highly technical job. (p. 64)

They describe a "myth chain" (p. 64) in which the story uses
a series of shots that convey cultural values:

First the camera dwells in close-up on an undefined, unillustrated
enemy. We look over the soldiers' shoulders, we share their position,
and thus their role as one-of-us, defending us and ours, is immedi-
ately identified. . . . "White hat" defends the fort/homestead/
wagon train against "black hat" or Indians. News reporting and
fiction use similar signs because they naturally refer to the same
myths in our culture. (pp. 64-65)

Ultimately, Fiske and Hartley explain a larger "mythology"
(p. 46), or cultural ideology, that the myths and myth chains
produce, in this case, "the relationship between major social
institutions and the individuals within them" (p. 46). The
military, economic and political institutions that exist in the
story are seen as "brave" though "doomed to failure" (p. 46).
As they explain, however,

the individuals working within these institutions are shown to be
acting as positively and as effectively as their institutional con-
texts will allow. Hence disillusionment with major institutions *as
such*, coupled with an undiminished respect for the individual,
would appear on the evidence of this typical [news story] to be a
crucial part of our contemporary mythology. (p. 47)

Himmelstein (1984) describes two other cultural myths reflected in the news. First is the "myth of the puritan ethic"
(p. 205), a myth that extols the values of hard work and
middle-class life while simultaneously questioning the values
of the underclass. If you work hard, so says the myth, you will
reap the benefits of The American Dream. The myth is reflected
not only in the stories that are covered but also in the star status
of television journalists who cover the stories. He writes,

Rarely do we get an adequate exploration or analysis of the increased
susceptibility of the lower socioeconomic classes to physical dan-

ger in the workplace or in inadequate housing, unsafe transportation, or lack of sufficient police protection outside the work environment; or of their desertion by the educational apparatus that teaches them at best how to cope in the technological world; at worst, how to fail. Instead, the success of those who have escaped these conditions through hard work is celebrated, while the basic structure of oppression is ignored. (p. 206)

Second, he describes the "myth of the rural middle landscape" (p. 218) that serves to "deflect attention from the chaos" of urban life,

the strong mature rural citizen coping with the evil world crashing all around him by maintaining pure country values, including the sanctity of the extended family and the value of hard work not for achievement, but for a higher moral purpose. (p. 218)

He argues that the danger here is that the urban life of American minorities, when contrasted with the myth of rural life, can unfairly signify a "moral" deficiency. Similarly, Richard Campbell (1991a, 1991b) describes the journalistic myth of middle America, a myth that pervasively affects news coverage:

Those who demand that the news media achieve "balance"—if not objectivity—must acknowledge that *balance* is a code word for *middle*—middle American values. These values are encoded into mainstream journalism—how it selects the news, where it places its beat reporters, who and how it promotes, how it critically reports and thereby naively supports government positions. (1991a, p. 75)

That "middle" is also apparent in what Hartley (1984) identifies as the "myth of marginality," which is reflected in the news media's coverage of events that are not part of the traditional, mainstream society in which journalism operates. He describes it as "that kind of thinking which makes sense of margins as irrelevant and peripheral." He adds, "It simply 'understands' that what happens at the edges either doesn't count or, worse, isn't there" (p. 121). Because African Americans and other minorities in America often find themselves outside the periphery of mainstream society, coverage of those communities may often reflect the "marginal" interest of the news media. As Essed (1991) points out,

> The application of white norms and values to blacks contains marginalizing and repressive elements. There is only a thin line between the use of dominant norms, rejection of "ethnic" behavior, and coercion to adapt. . . . Blacks can be tolerated as long as they remain marginal. (p. 196)

Stuart Hall (1973a) contends that the journalistic tenet of objectivity is itself a myth, "the absolute distinction between fact and value, the distinction which appears as a common sense 'rule' in newspaper practice" (p. 188). He says that myth is magnified by the "structure" (1973b, p. 86) of news production:

> The news is not only a cultural product: it is the product of a set of institutional definitions and meanings, which, in professional shorthand, is commonly referred to as *news values*. (p. 87)

Those values, he says, dictate a "status quo" production of news that reflects the "informal ideology" (p. 88) of journalism, which is based on "common sense understandings as to what constitutes the news in the newspaper discourse" (1973b, p. 179).

Hall is not alone in identifying "commonsense" practices as a potentially dangerous element of journalistic behavior. The insights about common sense of cultural anthropologist Clifford Geertz are often cited in discussions of its place in the news. Geertz (1983) writes,

> As a frame for thought, and a species of it, common sense is as totalizing as any other: no religion is more dogmatic, no science more ambitious, no philosophy more general. Its tonalities are different, and so are the arguments to which it appeals, but like them—and like art and like ideology—it pretends to reach past illusion to truth, to, as we say, things as they are. (p. 84)

The danger of the commonsense claim to truth is in its exclusion of those who live outside the familiar world it represents. In terms of news, this can mean a false sense of perspective. More than a half-century ago, Robert Park (1940) pointed out that the commonsense approach to news gave it a falsely scientific air and robbed it of any sense of history:

> News is not history because, for one thing among others, it deals, on the whole, with isolated events and does not seek to relate them to one another either in the form of causal or in the form of teleological sequences. . . . A reporter, as distinguished from a historian, seeks merely to record each single event as it occurs and is concerned with the past and future only in so far as these throw light on what is actual and present. (p. 675)

The common sense of the news process can also dictate what will (and will not be) covered. Tuchman (1978) explains that the *practical* nature of daily news gathering calls for a commonsense limitation of the selection process:

> The tempo of newswork, including covering a different story every day, mandates an emphasis on events, not issues. Events are concretely embedded in the web of facticity, the who, what, when, where, why, and how of the traditional news lead. Issues are not; they are based in analytic explanations of the everyday world as a socially experienced structure. For example, the idea and so the issue of institutionalized racism entails a description of social processes involving the interrelationship of a host of institutions and social problems; it eschews an examination of the prejudices of specific individuals. (p. 134)

Epstein (1973) further suggests that the production of television news can dictate a predetermined understanding of stories that strips them of real truth: "The entire process of reconstructing stories tends to fulfill preconceived expectations about how various events occur" (p. 180).

Other aspects of the journalistic process also call for a commonsense approach that can rob news of perspective, of truth. Campbell (1991a) believes,

> Common sense is typically represented in the familiar person-on-the-street interview. Someone, selected not for expertise but for ordinariness, is asked to voice an opinion about a newsworthy event or issue. When presented in the context of a news narrative, such

interviews take on the ambience of consensus. A single interview subject often stands in for a larger community of Middle-American viewers. Consequently, in stories presenting controversies, a lone interview or sound bite often determines which of the competing definitions of the situation is perceived as "correct," as common sense. (p. 116)

Though studies that examine myth and the commonsense meaning-making capacity of news are of primary importance to this study, it should be pointed out that qualitative researchers also utilize other useful approaches appropriate for application to studies of race and the news, some of which influenced this book. Van Dijk (1988a), for example, examines news via discourse analysis, looking at both the *text* and *context* of news in a cross-disciplinary approach that attempts to explain "how newsmakers actually *understand* what is going on, and how these understandings finally shape the news texts they produce" (p. 176).

Schudson (1978) approaches news from an historical perspective; like Hall, he views journalism's sacred claim to objectivity as ideology:

The belief in objectivity in journalism . . . is not just a claim about what kind of knowledge is reliable. It is also a moral philosophy, a declaration of what kind of thinking one should engage in, in making moral decisions. It is, moreover, a political commitment, for it provides a guide to what groups one should acknowledge as relevant audiences for judging one's own thoughts and acts. The relevant audiences are defined by institutional mechanisms. (p. 8)

Thornburn (1987), whose approach combines literary criticism and aesthetic anthropology, describes a "consensus narrative" that is subtly exhibited by the American television industry. Although he applies his criticism to TV fiction, his description of storytelling seems equally applicable to the "group journalism" process of TV news—reporters, camera operators, editors, producers, directors and others all working in conjunction to tell the day's stories:

The communal and collaborative dimension of consensus narrative helps to explain why . . . story forms are confined by the dominant pieties of the cultures they inhabit and explains their apparent lack of originality, their formulaic character. But it also explains their power to articulate what my old humanist teachers would have called the wisdom of the community. (p. 170)

Tuchman (1978), who *is* writing about news, describes a similar ideological consensus in the news process:

If an occurrence does not readily present itself as news easily packaged or in a known narrative form . . . it is dismissed by the limits inherent in the news frame.

To do otherwise, news professionals would have to question the very premises of the news net and their own routine practices. . . . They would have to recognize the inherent limitations of the narrative forms associated with the web of facticity. And they would have to come to terms with news as an indexical and reflexive phenomenon—a resource for social action in their own lives, in the lives of news consumers, and in the lives of the socially, politically, and economically powerful. (p. 215)

Tuchman suggests that the trappings of the journalistic process itself dictate an ideology, one that is so deeply imbedded in the news routine that it can make itself invisible.

This ideology may be as present in the news that audiences see as it is in that which they do not see. Lentz (1991) approaches news in terms of "strategic silence," or what the news leaves out. He contends that omissions by journalists can sometimes be more telling than what those journalists include in their stories:

The version of reality [journalists construct] relies upon the production of meanings based not only upon published content but upon ways in which some things are not "seen," or if seen, not recorded, as part of the social transaction between readers and creators of editorial matter. (p. 11)

The analyses that are summarized here come from a disparate range of approaches to media studies. Whether examining the media in terms of myth or common sense or through the use of some other technique or terminology, all of the research is intended to get at cultural meaning-making. Qualitative researchers have also had some success in determining the racial mythology and ideology that exists in America and can be reflected in the popular media. The next section of this chapter will examine some of those studies, as well as other research on contemporary racism.

▨ Contemporary Racism and the Mass Media

The qualitative research approach to racial attitudes reflected in the mass media is typified by sociologist Herman Gray's work. His 1986 article, "Television and the New Black Man: Black Male Images in Prime-Time Situation Comedies," addresses sitcoms but offers some direction appropriate for qualitative interpretation of racial myths in the news.

Gray points out that the television sitcom portrayals of black males during the 1983-1984 season—almost exclusively in middle-class surroundings—existed "in the absence of significant change in the overall position of black Americans as a social group" (p. 234). He found the dominant portrayal of blacks to be one of assimilation. That is, when audiences see African Americans on television it is nearly always within what Gray calls "the framework of assimilationist assumptions that emphasize racial harmony and an open society" (Gray, 1986, p. 238). Gray used shows from the mid-1980s, *Benson*, *Webster*, *Different Strokes* and *The Jeffersons*, but 1990s television reflects the same assimilationist notions in shows with majority African-American casts like *Fresh Prince of Bel-Air*, *Sinbad* and *Hangin' With Mr. Cooper*.

And why shouldn't prime-time television shows project a harmonious view of race relations in the United States? Wouldn't this appear to be a helpful approach, one in which the "melting pot" values of American society are reflected? As Gray (1986) concludes:

> Television's idealization of racial harmony, affluence and individual mobility is simply not within the reach of millions of black

Americans. . . . The present generation of black male images offers popular legitimation for a narrow and conservative definition of race relations and racial interaction. The major impact of this narrow conception is to deflect attention from the persistence of racism, inequality and differential power. (p. 239)

Gray's assumption that racism is alive and well in the United States is supported by research of contemporary racism. Hacker (1992) supplies recent statistics that clearly demonstrate the disparate existences of black and white Americans:

- Income for white families averages $36,915; for black families, $21,423.
- Although 8.8% of white Americans live in poverty, 31.9% of black Americans do.
- White unemployment is 4.1%; black unemployment is 11.3%.
- The infant mortality rate for white Americans is 8.1%; for black Americans, 16.5%.
- 24.4% of white Americans have attended 4 or more years of college; 12.7% of black Americans have.
- Black Americans make up less than 13% of the general population, but more than 45% of the prison population.

These statistics do not, however, tell the entire story of economics in black America. Wilson (1987) points out that the increased impoverishment felt by the minority underclass paradoxically coexists with increased wealth among the black middle and upper class. He writes,

The dilemma is that while the socioeconomic status of the most disadvantaged members of the minority population has deteriorated rapidly since 1970, that of advantaged members has significantly improved. (p. 109)

Wilson points to statistics from the 1970s and early 1980s— which reflect larger salaries for African American professionals and an increase in the number of blacks who attend college—in demonstrating the improved positions of economically successful minorities. But their success inadvertently bolsters the arguments of contemporary racists who point to it as evidence of equal opportunity, and—because of mythological under-standings of many Americans—the economic prosperity of a small number of minorities may be contributing to the economic detriment of other people of color.

Although the blatant bigotry of pre-civil rights America is largely (though not entirely) a thing of the past, contemporary racism theorists describe several forms of modern racism that have largely replaced the traditional and more overt form. "Symbolic racism" (Sears, 1988; sometimes called "modern racism"—see McConahay, 1986) is the form that accounts for the intolerance that still exists among many white Americans; symbolic racists are those who contend that they believe in equal rights for black Americans yet their behavior and politics indicate clearly antiblack attitudes. Symbolic racists tend to believe that blacks have achieved equality in American society and that they are now overly demanding in their push for justice (Sears, 1988). These beliefs would appear to explain the political success of ex-Ku Klux Klan Grand Wizard David Duke, who in 1990 garnered 60% of the white vote in Louisiana's U.S. Senate race. Writes Sears,

> Underlying racism continues to have an important political force.
> . . . Politicians can complain about demands and special favors
> and can insist that blacks need no special government action to
> achieve parity. (p. 80)

Similarly, Jhally and Lewis (1992) describe "enlightened racism" as the attitude of liberal whites who point to the social and economic success of a limited number of minorities in arguing that racism is not a factor in the failure of nonwhites to attain similar success. Jhally and Lewis interviewed a large number of white viewers of *The Cosby Show* before concluding that their perception of the show's fictional Huxtables enabled them to "combine an impeccably liberal attitude toward race with a deep-rooted suspicion of black people" (p. 110). They write,

> They are, on the one hand, able to welcome a black family into their
> homes; they can feel an empathy with them and identify with their

problems and experiences. They will, at the same time, distinguish
between the Huxtables and most other black people, and their
welcome is clearly only extended as far as the Huxtables. . . . They
reject bigotry based upon skin color, yet they are wary of most
(working class) black people. Color difference is okay, cultural
difference is not. (p. 110)

Another—and equally subtle—form of contemporary racism
has been described as "aversive racism" (Gaertner & Dovidio,
1986). Aversive racists are the liberal white Americans who are
outspoken in their support for civil rights for African Americans,
yet who tend to make antiblack decisions when no clear, "politically correct" decision is apparent. As Gaertner and Dovidio
explain,

Even if people genuinely attempt to reject the socially less desirable stereotypes and characterizations of blacks, it may be difficult for even the most well-intentioned white persons to escape
the development of negative beliefs concerning blacks and to
avoid feelings of superiority and relative good fortune over the
fact that they are white rather than black and are culturally
advantaged rather than disadvantaged. (p. 65)

Essed (1991) describes yet another form of contemporary
racism as "everyday racism," which "involves racist practices
that infiltrate everyday life and become part of what is seen
as 'normal' by the dominant group" (p. 288). She argues that
"dominant group members usually lack sensitivity to racism
in everyday life." She adds, "This is not surprising given that
. . . knowledge of racism is scarcely included in the formal
systems of transmission of knowledge, namely, the media and
education" (p. 285).

Though theorists on contemporary racism may not all use
the same terminology, it is evident that their research does
indicate the presence of prejudice and discrimination that lurk
in post-civil rights era America. As Bobo (1988) concludes:

The growing complexity and subtlety of racial attitudes and beliefs,
which the ideology of bounded racial change clearly reflects, derives
from a social context still characterized by considerable black-white

economic inequality, limited black political empowerment, extensive residential segregation by race, other historical trends and the influence of enduring cultural values and beliefs. (p. 109)

Contemporary forms of racism go a long way in explaining media portrayals of African Americans. *The Cosby Show*, its spinoffs and imitators are hardly a threat to the racial beliefs of the middle-class whites who make up the largest portion of those shows' audiences. Prime-time portrayals that offer us a harmonious view of race relations are easy choices for the middle- and upper-class white males who dominate the industry's top levels of decision making. The danger, however, is in the fact that the media portrayals can reflect contemporary racist attitudes and misrepresent minority life and culture.

Jhally and Lewis (1992) contend that *The Cosby Show* ultimately advanced the attitudes of enlightened racism—white viewers would cite their enjoyment of the program as evidence of their liberalism while simultaneously holding the belief that underclass minorities had only themselves to blame in not seizing American equal opportunity. Gray (1991) offers further evidence of the impact of television on this attitude by describing the "twin representations" of African Americans in fictional and nonfictional television (p. 304). He contrasts the upper-middle-class black life portrayed on *The Cosby Show* and the underclass black life portrayed in a 1985 PBS documentary entitled *The Vanishing Family: Crisis in Black America*. Race as it is portrayed on fictional television, according to Gray, is consistent with The American Dream, and

appeals to the utopian desire in blacks and whites for racial oneness and equality while displacing the persistent reality of racism and racial inequality or the kinds of social struggles and cooperation required to eliminate them. (p. 302)

The underclass black life of nonfictional TV, on the other hand, fails to

identify complex social forces like racism, social organization, economic dislocation, unemployment, the changing economy, or the

welfare state as the causes of the crisis in [the urban underclass]
community. (p. 300)

Gray concludes:

> The assumptions and framework that structure these representa-
> tions often displace representations that would enable viewers to
> see that many individuals trapped in the under class have the very
> same qualities [of hard work and sacrifices as seen on *Cosby*] but
> lack the options and opportunities to realize them. (p. 303)

So even though the images and themes reflected in prime
time shows with majority African American casts often mean
positive portrayals of minority life, the commonsense understandings they contribute to are not void of problematic meanings. Entman (1992) suggests that the frequency of African
American local television news anchors reinforces the racist
belief that Americans who are members of minority groups
have the same opportunities to succeed as white Americans,
and that those who don't succeed have only themselves to
blame. Entman also found that local television news reinforced
other aspects of modern racism. Of the stories he analyzed he
concluded:

> Local news implicitly traces the symbolic boundaries of the com-
> munity. The present exploration suggests that, in day-to-day
> coverage, blacks are largely cast outside those boundaries. . . .
> Crime reporting made blacks look particularly threatening, while
> coverage of politics exaggerated the degree to which black politi-
> cians (as opposed to white ones) practice special interest politics.
> These images . . . feed the components of modern racism, anti-
> black effect and resistance to blacks' political demands. (p. 342)

Van Dijk (1988b, 1988c) has found similar racism in study-
ing European coverage of ethnic minorities. In his study (1988c)
of newspaper headlines of Dutch newspapers, he found,

> As signals for and expressions of the ethnic situation, [the headlines]
> reduce ethnic groups and ethnic relations to a few prominent,
> attention-deserving, ethnic groupings, such as resident "foreigners"

and actually immigrating refugees. Almost all of these headlines spell "trouble" of some kind, whether because of the cause of crime, deviance, and social problems of resident minorities. Ethnic groups thus are relegated to second rank, dominated, passive position, and appear as responsible agents only in a stereotypical list of negative acts. (p. 260)

Often cited as the starting point in the research of race and the media is the report published by the Kerner Commission in 1968 that determined that the news media had "too long basked in a white world, looking out of it, if at all, with white men's eyes and a white perspective" (p. 389). Research since that time indicates that the dramatic changes called for by the commission have hardly been affected. Researchers consistently point to a pattern of news selection and coverage that represents the views and values of the homogeneous world of journalists. In his study of TV network news and weekly news magazine coverage, Gans (1979) observed, "News supports the social order of public, business, and professional, upper-middle-class, middle-aged, and white male sectors of society" (p. 61). He cites the "enduring values" of this social class—ethnocentrism, responsible capitalism, small-town pastoralism, moderatism— as the values that are propagated through news coverage.

The values shared by American journalists are not necessarily learned on the job; the hiring process can also reflect those values. Epstein (1973) noted the practice of news organizations hiring newsmen who "hold, or accept, values that are consistent with organizational needs, and reject others" (p. 43). Research has also indicated that journalists, once hired, tend to conform to the values of their news organizations as a means of socialization (Breed, 1960; Dimmick, 1974). As Breed noted, "The cultural patterns of the newsroom produce results insufficient for wider democratic needs" (p. 194).

The effects of hegemonic control of the media industry have been the source of considerable research. Lazarsfeld and Merton (1960) wrote that "by leading toward conformism and by providing little basis for a critical appraisal of society, the commercially sponsored mass media indirectly but effectively restrain cogent development of a genuinely critical outlook" (p. 503).

Bagdikian (1983) points to effects of America's capitalist economy on the news media, condemning the "homogenized" version of the news offered by the media, which he calls "diluted
of real meaning by apolitical and sterile context, homogenized
with the growth of monopoly" and "filled with frivolous material"
that "appeals largely to Americans with purchasing power"
(p. 206). He concludes:

> When the news is designed to exclude a third or a half of the
> population, it has sacrificed much of its standing as a democratic
> mechanism. And if it delivers accounts of events without relating
> them to the real world it has begun to fade as an important force
> in society. (p. 207)

The theory of "social responsibility," subscribed to by many
journalists and scholars as the role of the news media in modern
America, calls for a "truthful, comprehensive, and intelligent
account of the day's events in a context which gives them
meaning" and to project "a representative picture of the con-
stituent groups in society" (Siebert, Peterson, & Schramm, 1956,
p. 74). However, critics say news *practice* can differ from news
theory. Wilson and Gutiérrez (1985) argue that until major
policy changes are made in America's newsrooms, we can
expect more of the same. They write that "because America's
minority communities have not been reported on in the mainstream context by news media, their stories have not been told
adequately" (p. 141). They argue that news organizations have
not yet provided "an accurate assessment of ethnic minority
experience in the United States" (p. 141).

The dominant power structure is hesitant to make dramatic
changes. From the perspective of many newspaper editors,
minority coverage is viewed as adequate. As Rubin (1980) wrote
of his experience with defensive white journalists,

> Old timers and novices share a bad habit of pointing with pride
> to specific stories on minority problems to prove press interest.
> . . . What is lost to the news professionals and their audience is
> the fact that there is hardly any systematic reportage or analy-
> sis—hardly any followup on the most important stories, by way

of looking into related events and circumstances over a long
period of time. (p. 5)

The mass media has long been criticized for portrayals of
minorities, both for the stereotypes it helped reinforce and for
its propensity to ignore minority communities. Dates and
Barlow (1990) explain the dangers of those portrayals:

> Racial representations help to mold public opinion, then hold it
> in place and set the agenda for public discourse on the race issue
> in the media and in the society at large. Black media stereotypes
> are not the natural, much less harmless, products of an idealized
> popular culture; rather, they are more commonly socially con-
> structed images that are selective, partial, one-dimensional, and
> distorted in their portrayal of African Americans. Moreover, stereo-
> typed black images most often are frozen, incapable of growth,
> change, innovation, or transformation. (p. 5)

Although the outrageous stereotypes of pre-civil rights era
media may no longer exist, contemporary racism lurks beneath
the surface of many portrayals. As Hacker (1992) writes, "White
America still prefers its black people to be performers who
divert them as athletes and musicians and comedians" (p. 34).
The commonsense selection process of news organizations
often dictates coverage of "negative" minority news, while
"positive" stories about progress and success in minority communities tend to be shelved due to what journalists consider a
lack of newsworthiness. Writes Martindale (1986), "Clearly,
American journalism's emphasis on news as events, and as controversy, helps to produce a distorted picture of race relations
and of American blacks" (p. 40). And as Wilson and Gutiérrez
(1985) write, "In the absence of alternative portrayals and broadened coverage, one-sided portrayals and news articles could easily
become the reality in the minds of the audience" (pp. 41-42).
Mass media stereotypes are especially dangerous considering
the general lack of news coverage (or the lack of coverage with
a meaningful perspective) that has been documented in studies
of the news (Gist, 1990; Johnson & Sears, 1971; Martindale,
1990a, 1990b; Pease, 1989). What Johnson and Sears (1971)

wrote of the media in the aftermath of racial unrest in Los Angeles in 1965 rings equally true in 1992:

> Given that whites have very little direct personal knowledge of blacks, the mass media could potentially fill an important gap, communicating to whites the attitudes, feelings, life styles, and even the very existence of black people. Indeed, it is apparent that, without the aid of the media, most whites are likely to get very little information of any kind about blacks. (p. 702)

The "invisibility" of minorities in news coverage, as Rubin (1980) points out, "is not total, but what little is related about the diverse community is considered by many to be irrelevant or misleading" (p. 7).

The most common reason cited for news organizations' poor coverage of American minorities is the paucity of those minorities in America's newsrooms. After some increases in the number of minority journalists during the 1970s, more than half of the daily newspapers in the United States currently employ no minority journalists, and African Americans make up less than 5% of all daily newspaper journalists (American Society of Newspaper Editors [ASNE], 1992). Broadcast news organizations employ an equally low number of minorities, a number that also declined during the 1980s (Johnson & Bullard-Johnson, 1988). Like many black journalists, Philadelphia columnist Linda Wright Moore (1990) cites the absence of African Americans in the newsroom as the key to the distortion, or lack, of coverage. She admits that although African American journalists may "adopt the news values of the white institutions for which they work," she argues that—without them—"the mix of options to be considered in making . . . decisions on a day-to-day basis will be unnecessarily and perhaps irresponsibly restricted" (p. 23).

Minority journalists complain that newsroom policy often affects the news selection process, eliminating stories that don't fit the traditional news mold. Wilson and Gutiérrez (1985) write,

> A common complaint of ethnic minority reporters working in main-stream white newsrooms is the pressure of unwritten policy applied to their stories and "news angle" ideas. This is the manifestation of news being defined in terms of white majority perception. Both

minority and white reporters face sanctions when policy is violated. Sanctions include reprimand, loss of esteem among colleagues, and lessening of opportunity for upward mobility in the organization. (pp. 142-143)

Pulitzer Prize-winning journalist Nick Kotz (1979) points out an added difficulty for the minority journalist who is attempting to fit into a white newsroom:

Black journalists are consciously wracked by the dilemma W.E.B. DuBois posed seventy years ago. Blacks inevitably struggle with a "twoness," he wrote—with a desire to be loyal to themselves both as blacks and as Americans. (p. 28)

White editors are not likely to increase minority hiring until they are convinced that the increase will lead to better journalism. As Kotz says, editors must accept minority perspectives "not as intrusions of alien values, but as strengths that can enhance a newspaper's coverage" (p. 28).

The news media's interest in appealing to a middle-class white audience is not solely a reflection of the dominant value system that is at work. Because news organizations are businesses, their primary purpose is to make money; advertisers look for specific demographic audiences (those with the money to buy their products), and in the attempts by news organizations to attract those audiences, they tend to ignore the audiences that hold no interest for advertisers. Media executives "catering to the affluent, white majority might consciously avoid placing stories about minorities," writes Rubin (1980, p. 6), "due to their fear of losing the attractiveness of their media products vis-à-vis 'white readers coveted by advertisers.' "

Bagdikian (1983) points out that the audience being ignored is not a small one, noting that 50% of Americans live below the desirable income level sought by media advertisers:

Standard American newspapers and broadcasters would deny that they are racist. But their policies on reporting the news are indistinguishable from policies that would deliberately exclude minorities from news of their own society and normal news of minorities from the rest of the population. (p. 200)

Changes in this approach will come only from altruistic media managers, willing to sacrifice profit for improved news coverage and a sincere effort to live up to their social responsibility. As Wilson and Gutiérrez (1985) write, "The surveillance function of mass communication requires that news media inform society about the perspectives, aspirations, and contributions of all of its components" (p. 141).

Though the obvious effect of the stereotypes and invisibility of minorities is how it contributes to continued white racism, a final consideration is also worth raising—its effect on the self-image of minorities in America. As Gist (1990) writes,

> To what extent does journalistic bias influence the developing self-image of minority youth? While many minority youngsters do have strong, positive role models in their homes and communities, those who do not must rely to a greater extent on the secondary messages and images modeled in the mass media. To the extent that it is a common practice to portray African Americans most frequently in a negative light—criminals, drug addicts, etc.—or as positive examples from a negative context, strong signals are being sent to developing African American youth about what they can become. If a youngster wishes a more positive path, which models provide data? Again, for most minority subgroups, there are extremely few positive role models in the news; for African Americans, sports and entertainment are the fare. (p. 58)

In their overall perspective, American prime-time television and mainstream journalism appear to be telling audiences that America's unified melting pot is alive and well and that life for minority Americans will improve if members of those minority groups simply work hard and persevere. The popular media in America is generally telling us that racism does not exist, and that the economic, criminal and cultural problems that it causes have other roots. Rap music videos and films by African-American filmmakers like Spike Lee may be the only mass media that regularly address the issue of racism in a direct fashion and with a nonwhite, non-middle-class perspective.

The next three chapters of this study will attempt to interpret the "commonsense" racial myths embedded in the text of local television news. First, I will examine overt or "old-fashioned" elements of racism in the news and how minority invisibility marginalizes people of color. Second, I will examine traditional racist stereotypes that feed the notion of ethnics as different, as "other." Finally, I will examine the concept of assimilation in the news and how it contributes to the contemporary attitude of "enlightened racism."

CHAPTER 3

A Myth of Marginality
TRADITIONAL RACISM
AND THE NEWS

Along with the country as a whole, the press has too long basked in a white world, looking out of it, if at all, with white men's eyes and a white perspective.

—*Kerner Commission (1968, p. 389)*

The Kerner Commission concluded [that the news media] "failed to report adequately on the . . . underlying problems of race relations." . . . The statement remains just as relevant today.

—*Milton S. Eisenhower Foundation (1993, pp. 300–301)*

The application of white norms and values to blacks contains marginalizing and repressive elements. There is only a thin line between the use of dominant norms, rejection of "ethnic" behavior, and coercion to adapt.

—*Philomena Essed (1991, p. 196)*

M ost of the people who assisted me in compiling the videotaped newscasts for this study—family members, friends, former students, colleagues and other acquaintances in various cities around the country—returned the videotapes with short notes of encouragement. The words of one cousin, an engineer who lives near Milwaukee and taped that city's newscast for me, reflected an interesting perception of local television news coverage. The cousin, who knew that this study would deal with race and the news, wrote about the Milwaukee newscasts he had videotaped:

> I'm afraid you're going to see more on the rescue efforts accorded an injured canine than you are on race relations. . . .
>   Perhaps what is significant is the *lack* of coverage devoted to race relations. What does it say when the media spends more time on an injured, stray pooch than on injured, stray people? There's a good subject for exploration!

My cousin correctly sensed what researchers have discovered about coverage of minorities and minority issues by American news organizations. News coverage often ignores minorities and minority communities, keeping them at the periphery of American society and culture. Milwaukee's WITI did indeed give lengthy coverage on January 18 and 19 to the rescue of an injured dog. On those same dates, several of the other newscasts viewed for this study included stories about injured animals, including New Orleans's WWL, which committed extensive resources and airtime to the rescue of a duck whose bill had become stuck in a plastic twist-tie.

There are many factors that contribute to local television journalism's penchant for covering the frivolous. First, the primary purpose of news organizations is to make money and, in the minds of some local TV news executives, stories about wounded animals are more likely to draw viewers than thoughtful coverage of the day's vital issues (like, for instance, race relations). Second, the production process of television news— the daily scramble for reporters and camera crews to get stories, the editing and scripting of videotaped events to meet stringent deadlines, the cosmetic appeal of the on-air talent, the intensity of "live" television—often dictates coverage that is more amusing than insightful. Media critic Ron Powers (1977) once wrote that the process forces television journalists to "live with built-in shackles that prevent them from digging beneath the surface of predictable events and acting as true ombudsmen for viewers" (p. 67).

The news that audiences see, then, may not always be the thorough, accurate and "socially responsible" reflection of American life that news organizations would ideally depict, especially for nonwhite Americans. As Wilson and Gutiérrez (1985) argue, "A lot of work remains before a semblance of balance is attained that will provide an accurate assessment of ethnic minority experience in the United States" (p. 141).

Although the overall focus of this study will be to examine more subtle reflections of contemporary notions of racism in the news, the purpose of this chapter is to examine local TV news coverage for evidence of lingering vestiges of traditional racism, the sort of overt racism that many Americans consider a thing of the past. First, I will discuss the underrepresentation of minorities in the news, which contributes to a marginalization of the lives and interests of people of color. Second, I will closely examine coverage of events on two newscasts—one from Hattiesburg, MS, the other from Minneapolis/St. Paul, MN—that seem to reflect the persistence of traditional racism. I argue here that the general invisibility of minorities, especially when combined with occasional overtly racist coverage, contributes to a mythological understanding of minorities as *marginal*, as less significant and less valued members of society.

"Old-Fashioned" Racism and Minority Invisibility

McConahay (1982) and Sears (1988) use the phrase "old-fashioned racism" to describe the traditional bigotry associated with pre-Civil War ethnic stereotypes, pro-segregationist attitudes and open racial discrimination. Traditional racism regards white Americans as superior, as privileged. It considers people of color to exist outside of mainstream society; it marginalizes minority group members, if not ignoring them all together. Certainly much of this type of racism has been eradicated in the United States since the days of the civil rights movement, but it is not gone completely. Occasionally it rears its head—a major league baseball executive makes disparaging remarks about African American ballplayers, a former Ku Klux Klan grand wizard gathers broad political support on a scarcely concealed antiblack platform.

There was no striking evidence of intentional, blatant bigotry in the nearly 40 hours of news programming that I examined for this study. Indeed, all 28 stations whose programs I viewed that were broadcast on the date of the Martin Luther King, Jr. holiday carried coverage in tribute to the slain civil rights leader. And African American journalists made up 11% of the news anchors and reporters who appeared on the programs[1] (see Appendix B). In general, the coverage that I viewed reflects that most American journalists are at least somewhat sensitive to racial matters, and that many news organizations see a need for hiring minority journalists.

But the legacy of hundreds of years of overt racism is not easily vanquished. Most of the research that deals with race and the news has documented the underrepresentation of minority journalists in America's newsrooms (e.g., ASNE, 1992; Stone, 1988a, 1988b; Kerner Commission, 1968; U.S. Commission on Civil Rights, 1977). Eleven percent of the journalists seen on camera in this study were African American, a percentage that is roughly consistent with national statistics on minority employment in television news; research indicates that 13.3% of TV journalists are members of ethnic minority groups (Stone, 1988b). But that number has been on the decline since the early 1980s, and those numbers are probably misleading in terms of the overall representation of minority journalists and of their impact on news coverage. Studies have found that minorities are largely employed either in high profile, on-camera positions (Schultz, 1988; Stone, 1988a) or as camera operators (Stone, 1988a) rather than in editorial decision-making capacities. Only 4% of local television news directors are people of color, and whites hold 92% of the supervisory jobs that usually lead to those positions, such as assistant news director, assignment editor or executive producer (Stone, 1988a).

The research that deals with how news about minorities is actually covered—much of it looking at print coverage—has found that minority communities continue to be largely ignored and/or stereotyped in news media portrayals (e.g., Entman, 1990, 1992; Gist, 1990; Martindale, 1990a, 1990b; Pease, 1989). A 1971 study of the underrepresentation of minorities in the news media argued,

> By helping to perpetuate black invisibility, [the news media embody]
> institutional racism and [fail] to combat the white public's igno-
> rance about it. (Johnson & Sears, p. 718)

That same argument may be equally applicable to today's news
coverage. As Pease (1989) concluded,

> Minorities seem to have made little progress since 1965 in terms
> of having their voices and concerns heard, their problems dis-
> cussed, their triumphs and sorrows reported and their opinions
> considered. (p. 34)

Although my approach to this research is a qualitative one
and I chose not to analyze the content of stories quantitatively,
evidence of minority invisibility was conspicuous in viewing
the newscasts videotaped for this study. Although the stations
devoted differing amounts of coverage to the King holiday, few
covered any stories about minorities or minority communities
on the following day's broadcasts; minorities rarely served as
on-camera news sources, and feature reports (other than those
included in the sports segments of the programs—a topic that
will be dealt with in the next chapter) virtually always highlighted white people and activities in white communities. And
though 11% of the anchors and reporters were African American, other minorities were overwhelmingly underrepresented
(see Appendix B).

Of the hundreds of feature stories (e.g., profiles, community
activities, animal injuries, etc.) that were aired during these
newscasts, only one solely highlighted a person of color: Des
Moines, IA's KCCI carried a story on its January 19, 6 p.m.
newscast about the retirement of an African American prison
warden who had been credited with restoring order at a troubled penitentiary. Some feature stories did focus on integrated
groups, and minority existence was evident in coverage of some
health and finance related reporting. But the newscasts' feature
stories appeared to exhibit the same pattern that has been found
in content analysis research—little coverage of the nonwhite
community and the consistent use of white sources in stories
on topics that affect audience members of all colors.[2]

Evidence of minority invisibility was equally conspicuous in local news coverage of the January 20 presidential inauguration. Although the stations sent a total of 25 reporters to Washington, D.C., to cover the installation of President Bill Clinton, all but 1 of those reporters were white. And of the 28 stories that "regionalized" the inauguration by covering local people and groups in attendance at the inauguration, only 2 primarily featured ethnic minority sources: St. Louis's KSDK carried on its 5 p.m. newscast a short "reader," accompanied by videotape, about a troop of black Marine veterans who had been invited to the event, and San Francisco's KPIX covered two reformed black gang members who had been invited to attend. Though some racially integrated groups were covered—a high school marching band from Virginia, an elementary school history class from Lafayette, LA—the localized coverage of the inauguration contradicted the testimony of a Minneapolis reporter who described the "diversity" of the crowds present at the inaugural events and how well everyone was "getting along." Rather than any sense of diversity, most stations offered coverage of what appeared to be all-white groups—a Minnesota polka band, a group of Tennesseeans from Vice President Al Gore's hometown who called themselves "Al's Pals," Ohio Democratic Party leaders—and interviews were conducted with white participants.

Even though African American and other minorities more commonly appeared in the "hard news" stories viewed for this study (often in the form of stereotypes, which will be discussed in the next chapter), many of those stories also appeared to exclude minority community considerations. For instance, in coverage of the harsh weather that affected Los Angeles and Phoenix on January 18 and 19, 17 of the 18 weather victims interviewed by reporters on stations in the two cities were white. The minority populations of Phoenix—about 28% (U.S. Department of Commerce, 1990)—and Los Angeles—38%—are substantial, so although Los Angeles's KNBC anchor Kelly Lange described the situation as "a nightmare everywhere you look," the stations did not seem to look everywhere. Did the storms somehow not affect ethnic minority communities?

Some of the disparity of coverage may have as much to do with class as race. The literature review for this study describes the severe economic differences between white and black Americans.

It is possible that fewer people of color attended inaugural events simply because of the cost of getting there. And perhaps the severe weather in Arizona and California had a more dramatic and newsworthy impact in wealthier, whiter neighborhoods. Certainly the palatial ocean-front houses teetering on the edges of washed-out cliffs made for sensational pictures.

But class differences cannot entirely explain the pattern of minority invisibility that appeared to be present in this study and has been described by quantitative researchers. It is just as likely that the process of news selection and coverage, when dictated in overwhelmingly white newsrooms, will entail coverage that reflects white existence. As Gist (1990) discovered in her examination on the impact of majority culture domination of the news, news organizations showed a "significantly greater tendency" to present

> a balanced picture of non-minority subjects, more positive or neutral stories from positive or neutral contexts, such as weddings, home purchases, political and community activities, for instance. In other words, unlike coverage of minorities, . . . presentation of whites [is] not restricted to negative examples or sports/entertainment, but portrayed them in an extensive variety of mainstream activities. (p. 54)

The Kerner Commission (1968) argued 25 years ago that the news media

> repeatedly, if unconsciously, reflects the biases, the paternalism, the indifference of white America. This may be understandable but it is not excusable in an institution that has the mission to inform and educate the whole of society. (p. 66)

There have been changes in the past 25 years. African American journalists appear in prominent roles on local television news programs. Coverage of events like the Martin Luther King, Jr. holiday provides evidence that minority communities are not totally ignored. But those changes may be masking the fact that the kinds of changes advised by the Kerner Commission, which called for coverage that placed events into "meaningful perspective" (p. 389), have not taken place. The general lack of coverage of minority issues and minority communities by local television news contributes to a sense of "otherness" about nonwhite Americans; their existence is not ignored as it was 25 years ago, but the lack of perspective, of depth, can dictate news coverage that continues to advance a dangerous perception of minority life, what Hartley (1984) calls a "myth of marginality." Coverage that overlooks the complexities of existence in minority communities while unwaveringly doting on white life and majority culture reflects a common sense about minority life that places nonwhites in the margins, outside of mainstream American society. As Hartley writes,

> It is that kind of thinking which makes sense of margins as irrelevant and peripheral when they can equally be understood as disruptive and threatening. It is mythical thinking because it "magically resolves" the ambiguity of marginality. It simply "understands" that what happens at the edges either doesn't count or, worse, isn't there. (p. 121)

This study does not intend to establish a quantitative pattern of minority underrepresentation in the news. Other studies have provided the kind of data that reflects a sort of marginalization through omission. But the "myth of marginality" that Hartley describes is also occasionally evident in news coverage that reflects a common sense that is decidedly white and that contributes to an understanding of minorities as a peripheral part of mainstream American society. The approach of the rest of this chapter will be an interpretive one; that is, I will be closely "reading" news stories as "texts." I will examine three stories that appear to reflect minority marginalization and the persistence of overt racism in the news.

▓ "Everyday" Racism and News Coverage

Case One: Mississippi Celebrations

The first two stories to be analyzed come from the 6 p.m. news program broadcast on WDAM-TV, Monday, January 18. WDAM is an NBC affiliate located in Hattiesburg, MS, and serving the Hattiesburg-Laurel, MS, market—listed as the 164th "ADI" (area of dominant interest) market in the United States (*Broadcasting*, 1992). Hattiesburg is a city of nearly 42,000, with an African American population of about 40% (U.S. Department of Commerce, 1990). Laurel is a city of about 19,000, with an African American population of about 48%. Perhaps more representative of WDAM's audience, however, are the demographics of the two counties in which those cities are found. The total population of Jones and Forrest Counties is about 130,000. African Americans make up about 28% of that population.

On its January 18 broadcast, WDAM ran 12 news stories, ranging from 15 seconds to 2 minutes in length, as well as a weather forecast and a sports report. WDAM journalists who appeared on-screen included two white anchors, a white sports anchor, a white meteorologist and two white field reporters. Stories ranged from a murder in Laurel to problems with the Jones County jail to disaster relief for a tornado-damaged area. The broadcast also included two stories that will serve as the basis for this textual analysis. The first, which ran for about 27 seconds about 8 minutes into the program, described a parade in Laurel in honor of that day's Martin Luther King, Jr. holiday (see Appendix C for a complete transcript of the story). The second, which directly followed that story and ran for about 60 seconds, described a local tribute to Confederate General Robert E. Lee (see Appendix D).

For now, I will ignore the peculiar juxtaposition of these two stories—one related to our nations's most prominent civil rights leader, the other to the commander of the Southern forces during the Civil War. Instead, I will first examine the King parade story in its own right, then the Lee tribute story. Following that, I will analyze the juxtaposition and compare the station's coverage of the two stories.

In semiotic terms, we can look at the stories on several levels of signification. Barthes (1957/1972) analyzed images and words on many tiers, among them denotation, connotation and myth. He described denotation as the first order of signification; in this case, the words we hear and the images we see on the television screen can be described in their most overt terms.

On the denotative (or "signified") level, the King parade story was handled as a "reader" by anchor Bob Noonan; that is, as Noonan reads the story, the audience first sees a medium (chest-up) shot of the anchor, then "actuality" footage from the parade. No reporter is seen at the parade site, and no interviews are conducted with participants. The audience is told that about 75 people participated in the march, and the long shot (from a distance—an "establishing" shot) of the parade indicates that this is probably an accurate estimate. In the shots that follow we see that many of the marchers appear to be children, and all appear to be black. The audience is told that the parade organizers "hope the commemoration will make young people more aware of [King's] legacy and bring blacks as well as whites together."

On the second level of signification, connotation, the story takes on ideological meaning as well. The story could be "read" as a symbol of the continuance of the civil rights movement, King's hopes for an integrated America, promises of an American future that does not discriminate, an end to bigotry. An honor guard leads the parade carrying an American flag, a symbol of this country's sense of freedom and justice. These connotations reflect what Campbell (1991a) has described as a "middle-American" mythology; in that way, the story reflects a commonsense notion—or, in Barthes's words, "the naturalization" (p. 131)— of the American melting pot. The images could also be seen as a reflection of what Mixon (1989) describes as New South mythology, reflecting a sense of a post-civil rights era South that is a tolerant and progressive place where equality and fairness prevail, "a land that [is] rich, just, and triumphant" (p. 1114). Hall (1980) would describe these readings as "dominant" or "preferred"; that is, from the point of view of WDAM's journalists and many of the station's viewers, the images here would reflect a majority culture understanding of those images.

But other connotations can also be read into the story, those that Hall would describe as "negotiated" or "oppositional." An observer who rejects the coverage's "preferred" codes might question the "dominant" interpretation: If King's dream of racial unity is alive, why are all of the marchers black? And why are all of the WDAM journalists white? Although the script would indicate the journalists' commonsense acceptance of the value of "bringing blacks as well as whites together," the fact is that Laurel, MS, and most other American cities are largely geographically and economically divided along racial lines. In the story,

no African Americans are interviewed. With only white journalists on camera the station's coverage ritualizes the myth of
marginality. Although nearly 30% of the viewers in WDAM's
market are African Americans, the coverage suggests a sense of
"otherness" about the black people who are participating in the
march, implying, as Hartley says, that "what happens at the
edges . . . doesn't count" (p. 121). Or, as Essed (1991) describes
one aspect of "everyday" racism, "Blacks can be tolerated as long
as they remain marginal" (p. 196). The myth of the New South,
writes Mixon, "fail[s] to reflect reality adequately" (p. 1114).

The commonsense/dominant culture mythology at work in
the King parade story is more clearly evident in the Lee tribute
story that follows. On the denotative level, we see a medium
shot of anchor Whitney Vann who offers this transition from
King to Lee: "While each of the fifty states honored the life and
legacy of Dr. Martin Luther King today, thousands of Southerners paid tribute as well to Robert E. Lee." As she reads, we see
a close-up of a portrait of Lee, a full (head-to-toe) shot of six
men in Civil War uniforms firing guns into the air, a close-up
of the base of a statue that reads, "TO THE MEN AND WOMEN
OF THE CONFEDERACY," a full shot of five people who are
apparently attending the tribute, a full shot of a woman in Civil
War-era clothing placing a wreath at the foot of the statue, then
a full shot of the sculpted soldier who is on top of the statue,
possibly Lee.

Vann says that Lee's birth date is "one of several special days
including Confederate Memorial Day and Jefferson Davis' birthday observed nearly 130 years after the end of the Civil War."
She then tells the audience that "a Hattiesburg member of the
Sons of Confederate Veterans says Robert E. Lee is well deserving
of the honor."

Next we see a full shot of a man identified in a graphic as
Rick Forte. He is seated on a couch, apparently in a room in his
home that is filled with Civil War memorabilia. He wears a T-shirt
that displays a Confederate battle flag. A full shot shows an
unidentified reporter who is taking copious notes while seated
on a chair next to Forte. A close-up of Forte speaking remains
until the end of the story. He says, "[Lee] just stood for what a
Southern gentleman stood for and what a soldier stood for—
honor, you know, land, your home, honor, family. He stood for

that." Vann's voice-over concludes the piece: "Rick Forte is the man who discovered skeletal remains designated and reburied in 1979 as the official unknown Confederate soldier."

Mythic connotations can be read in both the language that is used in the story and in the images we see on camera. The anchor links King and Lee without acknowledging the obvious irony—King, the ultimate symbol of black America's push for equality; Lee, commander of the Southern army that fought to maintain the enslavement of black Americans. We are told that "thousands" of Southerners paid tribute to Lee, and that "for decades" this and other "special days" are observed "nearly 130 years after the end of the Civil War." The anchor's common-sense explanation of the tribute to Lee and her introduction to the story's key source—"a Hattiesburg member of the Sons of Confederate Veterans says Robert E. Lee is well deserving of the honor"—lend legitimacy to the middle-American/Southern values he espouses in his account of Lee's symbolic worth: "He just stood for what a Southern gentleman stood for and what a soldier stood for—honor, you know, land, your home, honor, family. He stood for that."

His words suggest that what he says is obvious, a truth that cannot be questioned: The "just" in his "he *just* stood for" implies an implicit acceptance of his explanation of Lee's symbolism. The "you know" that is inserted in his list of the values he associates with Lee sounds less like a nervous hesitation than an appeal to the reporter who sits across from him, perhaps to the audience, that his interpretation is manifest: "*we* know." The attributes he cites echo some of the "enduring values" described by Gans (1979)—like ethnocentrism and small-town pastoralism—who argued that news supports a "social order" (p. 61) of white, male hegemony. By tying together the concepts of the Southern gentleman and soldier with honor (which comes up twice in the list), land, "your home" and family, Forte's version of Lee's symbolic value seems to preclude an understanding of these values outside of that realm. He conjures up a Southern myth of family life and rural existence that, as Sharp (1989) points out, hardly fits today's South:

> In recent years southern families have experienced much the same rates of change as families throughout the rest of the nation, with

growing numbers of divorces, single-parent families, and two-income couples seeking childcare. Also, the region is no longer predominantly rural, residents are very mobile and most adults maintain frequent contacts only within the nuclear family and with parents and siblings. (p. 1105)

But Forte's version is authenticated by a sort of natural acceptance on the part of the two journalists who appear in the story, the anchor and the unidentified reporter. What Bobo (1988) calls the "enduring cultural values and beliefs" that contribute to "the ideology of bounded racial change" (p. 109) become the commonsense understanding of Lee's symbolism. In a final legitimization of Forte as a news source, the anchor concludes the story by describing Forte as "the man who discovered skeletal remains designated and reburied in 1979 as the official unknown Confederate soldier." In what Thornburn (1987) calls "consensus narrative," the story reflects "the wisdom of the community" (p. 170).

The images we see also contribute to that narrative. The soldiers firing rifles into the air in salute and the crowd watching as a wreath is placed at the foot of the Confederate memorial reflect community support. The Confederate flag that appears on Forte's T-shirt becomes a reflection of moral virtue; never mind the fact that it is the symbol of choice for white supremacists. A "cutaway" shot shows the unidentified white reporter sitting next to Forte busily taking down Forte's words into his notebook, adding increased legitimacy to Forte's "commonsense" perception of the tribute to Lee.

In running the King parade and Lee tribute stories side by side, and in linking them in the anchor's transition between the two, the program suggested a parallel—two stories about Americans celebrating the lives of American heroes. But a comparison of the coverage of the two stories raises further questions about the mythic nature of race and the news. Park (1940) argues that news robs events of historical meaning, placing isolated events in a vacuum. In this case, the stories' lack of historical perspective dictates a very narrow, commonsense understanding of the events.

Semiological analysis allows for examination of these texts within a more immediate context of associations. As Seiter (1987) writes, "Semiotics argues that the meaning of every sign derives in part from its relationship to others with which it is associated in the same sign system" (p. 36). Through paradigmatic (sets of similar signs) and syntagmatic (sign sequence) analysis, we can examine the two stories within the context of the "sign system" of local television news. A paradigmatic examination of the stories calls for a look at the coverage in terms of language and visual imagery. The syntagmatic approach allows us to look at the juxtaposition of the two stories as part of a sequential, meaning-making chain.

Both stories ran on January 18, the day set aside as the national Martin Luther King, Jr. holiday. Although it is not mentioned, the Lee tribute was actually a day early—Lee's birth date is January 19. On a paradigmatic level, the Lee tribute is granted more detailed and salient coverage, in both the language used to describe the events and in the allotment of the station's resources. The King parade story ran first, but only for about 27 seconds—less than half the time allotted for the Lee tribute story. The coverage indicates that the station sent only a camera operator to cover the King parade, but sent both a reporter and camera operator to cover the Lee tribute. No interviews are conducted by participants in the King parade, leaving only WDAM's white journalists to explain its significance. Although we are told that the parade was "one of a series of holiday events in Laurel," this is the only one that we see. The parade, described as including "about 75 participants" and illustrated primarily from a distant camera angle, looks small and somewhat disjointed.

In the coverage of the Lee tribute, we are told that "thousands of Southerners paid tribute" to Lee, although we see a total of only about 10 on camera. There are no long shots of the tribute at the Confederate monument, so we never get a sense of the size of the crowd in attendance. What we do see is a series of full shots, one showing a rifle-firing salute, another showing a woman placing a wreath at the foot of a statue, another of 5 people in attendance. The impression that the crowd shot creates—coupled with the anchor's explanation that thousands of Southerners celebrated Lee's birthday (though she did not mention that they were a day early)—is that many more may also be in attendance. The interview with Forte that concludes the story grants it further prominence. A spokesperson for the "thousands," Forte becomes the commonsense voice of middle-America and the mythical South.

The anchor tells us that "for decades" Lee's birthday has been "commemorated throughout the South," evoking Old South tradition and legacy. The description of the King parade in small-town Laurel, MS, pales in comparison. The American flag carried in the King parade—perhaps a symbol of a New South, the integrated and open-minded place of contemporary Southern mythology—flutters in ironic contrast to the Confederate stars and bars on Forte's chest.

How is it that the coverage of the Lee tribute was granted more prominence than the celebration of the national Martin Luther King, Jr. holiday? A cynic might wonder if the Lee tribute was a media event intentionally staged a day before Lee's birth date as a distinctly white celebration to counteract the impact of the commemoration of America's most prominent black leader.

A syntagmatic reading of the two stories fails to support a sense of journalistic neutrality about the coverage. The juxtaposition and coverage of stories about these two heroes certainly raises questions about the racial sensitivity of WDAM's journalists. Although both men may merit tribute for the contributions they made to their causes, the symbolic contradiction inherent in those two causes is a blatant one. It is likely that those journalists intended no offense. Research of contemporary racism describes the "aversive" form of racism as one in which

> people who have developed a value system that maintains it is wrong to discriminate against a person because of his or her race, who reject the content of racial stereotypes, who attempt to disassociate negative feelings about blacks from their self-concepts, but who nonetheless cannot entirely escape cultural and cognitive forces. (Gaertner & Dovidio, 1986, p. 66)

So despite the best intentions of the white journalists, who may have seen the two stories as balanced and representative, their coverage reflects, at best, insensitivity and, at worst, overt racism that marginalizes African American life. In describing "everyday" racism, Essed (1991) offers this possible explanation: "Dominant group members usually lack sensitivity to racism in everyday life. They have little understanding of the problem because they are not confronted, on a regular basis, with critical views of race and ethnic relations" (p. 285).

Case Two: Minnesota Spearfishing

KARE-TV is an NBC affiliate serving the Minneapolis-St. Paul, MN, market—the country's 13th largest (*Broadcasting*, 1992). The twin cities total about 640,000 residents; whites make up almost 80% of that population, Native Americans about 5% (U.S. Department of Commerce, 1990).

On its January 19 broadcast, KARE ran 14 news and feature stories as well as weather and sports reports. Eight KARE journalists—two anchors, four reporters, a meteorologist and a sports anchor—appeared on camera during the broadcast, all of them white. News stories covered topics ranging from a shooting in North Minneapolis to the attempted rescue of a farm accident victim to an increase in state gasoline taxes. KARE lead off the newscast with its longest story of the evening, a 3-minute, 15-second account of a fishing rights controversy pitting Minnesota's sports fishermen against a Native American tribe; that story will serve as the basis for this chapter's final textual analysis (see Appendix E for a complete transcript of the story).

On a denotative level, the story was handled as a news "package" by the KARE crew; that is, the coanchors and a reporter contribute information, and we see "actuality" videotape as well as "live" coverage of the reporter at the Minnesota Capitol Building. The story unfolds like this:

First, we see a long shot of snow-covered Lake Mille Lacs in the daylight, then a cut to a medium shot of an unidentified man—apparently a Native American—spearing a fish from a boat at night. Anchor Paul Magers reads, "A frozen blanket of ice covers the waters of Lake Mille Lacs, but this serene setting is the centerpiece of Minnesota's hottest controversy. The issue? Native American spearfishing." Next we see coanchors Magers and Pat Miles on the set, and Miles explains that the agreement reached by state officials and a Chippewa Indian group is one that "some anglers fiercely hate." We are then sent to reporter Dennis Stauffer at the Capitol for "the details." He explains that the agreement is "showing no signs of calming the controversy."

Next we see videotape of two unidentified anglers—apparently white sports fishermen—one pulling a large fish out of a hole in the ice on a rod and reel while the other assists. Stauffer explains that Lake Mille Lacs is "Minnesota's premiere trophy fishing lake" and that the agreement, according to the commissioner of the Division of Natural Resources, will protect sports fishing. The white Department of Natural Resources (DNR) commissioner is then seen seated at the head table of a news conference; he sits next to a Native American man who apparently negotiated the agreement with the state. A graphic is shown to illustrate a 6,000-acre "treaty zone" that gives the Mille Lacs Indian reservation exclusive access to what appears to be about 8% of the lake. A second graphic outlines the terms of the agreement, which Stauffer describes. It allows for Indian netting and spearing of fish in the treaty zone, apportions the Indian harvest to the limit on the entire lake and calls for the state to pay the tribe $10 million and cede 7,500 acres of state land to the tribe.

We then see the DNR commissioner at the news conference explaining that, without the agreement, the state could lose a lawsuit to the tribe: "We could lose as much as half the fish in Mille Lacs Lake," he says, "and if that were the case I think it would have a tremendous impact on sport fishing, tourism and local economy." We then see videotape, the same footage shown at the top of the story, that shows a fish being speared. Next Stauffer tells us that the DNR commissioner had cited a Wisconsin lawsuit that granted Indian tribes 50% of the fish in a lake that borders on Minnesota. A graphic shows that a 1837 treaty that was upheld in that case also covered the Mille Lacs Lake area.

Next we see videotape of a group of about 75 men who are apparently protesting the agreement, some holding signs reading "No nets" and "Governor Carlson—We need your help." Stauffer tells us that "critics, which include sports and tourist groups, say the Indians gave up their rights long ago under subsequent treaties and that Minnesota would win in court." Next is a close-up of Bud Grant, the former head coach of the Minnesota Vikings football team. A long, low angle shot of Grant shows that he is seated in front of a wall full of Viking memorabilia, most prominently the number 10 jersey of Fran Tarkenton, once the team's star quarterback. Stauffer tells us that Grant is the honorary chairman of the Save Mille Lacs Association. Grant says, "I think there is a right and a wrong. Why should one group of people be allowed to do something another group of people cannot do? Why should they have exclusive rights?"

Finally, we see Stauffer again in the assembly room of the Capitol Building. He explains that both the Mille Lacs tribe and the state legislature will have to approve the agreement before it will become law. Then we see the coanchors back in the studio, watching Stauffer on a large monitor. Coanchor Magers asks Stauffer, "Is the tribe happy with it as well?" Stauffer says the Indian negotiator had supported it, and that the tribe is more likely to approve the treaty than is the state legislature. Coanchor Miles then asks if the agreement has the potential "to become the most controversial issue before the state legislature this year?" Stauffer tells her, "It certainly has the potential to generate the most sparks around here."

On a connotative level, the story takes on mythic meaning not unreminiscent of traditional "cowboy and Indian" movies. The magnitude of the conflict between the Native American tribe and the white sportsmen (represented on camera by the ice fishermen, the protestors and spokesman Bud Grant) is accentuated in the words the journalists use throughout the story. The "headlines" that preceded that evening's newscast made the first reference to "the Lake Mille Lacs controversy." In introducing the story, anchor Paul Magers calls the issue "Minnesota's hottest controversy." Coanchor Pat Miles then says the white sportsmen "fiercely hate" the proposed agreement. Reporter Stauffer says the agreement shows "no sign of calming the controversy." The theme is repeated at the end of the story when Miles asks Stauffer if the issue is potentially "the most controversial issue before the state legislature," and he says it "has the potential to generate the most sparks." The story's language draws clear battle lines.

The narrative continues to evoke Western film mythology by posturing the Indians as the "bad guys." A Native American source to offer the tribe's point of view is never heard, thereby marginalizing that point of view; as in the old movies, the audience is never asked to consider a nonwhite understanding of the story. Three white journalists report on the events, a white state official describes the agreement, a throng of white protesters represents the dissatisfaction of "sports fishing" enthusiasts and local hero Bud Grant, a white man, serves as the commonsense champion of their cause. "There is a right and a wrong," he says.

The story's visual imagery further summons the film stereotypes of Native Americans. Trimble (1988) describes one stereotyped view of Native Americans as "untamed, innocent, . . . pure lovers of nature" (p. 188). Twice in the story we see the same "actuality" footage to illustrate spearfishing. No one is identified, but the tape—which lasts only about 8 seconds— would appear to be from the station's files because the water is not frozen. It is dark, and a man in a boat takes one poke with a long wooden spear into the water, which is illuminated by someone holding a flashlight. He pulls out the spear, on which is impaled a wriggling fish. Then we briefly see two men carrying their canoe to shore.

Both times we see it, we do not hear the sound on the tape. The first time it is shown, anchor Paul Magers is introducing the story as "Minnesota's hottest controversy . . . Native American spearfishing." The second time we see it, reporter Dennis Stauffer is describing a lawsuit in Wisconsin that upheld Native American fishing rights. The only other Native American we see in the story is the tribe member who negotiated the agreement seated at the press conference. He is never identified, nor do we hear from him. In the absence of any other image of tribal life, the spearfishing videotape becomes the central characterization of Native American existence. Although it may seem appropriate (common sense) to use the tape to illustrate spearfishing, it also contributes to the kind of historical robbery described by Parks (1940) in which news coverage fails to place single events into meaningful context. The audience never is given a sense of why the Wisconsin court, in a similar case, upheld Native American fishing rights, which might go a long way in giving the story some historical perspective. And the audience never hears from a Native American who could articulate that perspective.

Syntagmatically, the spearfishing video also works as a binary opposite of the brief "sports fishing" tape seen during the story. As Stauffer explains that Mille Lacs is "Minnesota's premiere

trophy fishing lake," we watch as a large fish is slowly pulled
by rod and reel from a hole in the ice by one man, as another
bends down and grabs it. We briefly hear the sound on the
tape, and a jolly angler shouts, "There we go! Ha! Ho!" The
contrast between spearfishing and "trophy fishing" furthers
the story's white, commonsense perception of the use and
function of America's natural resources: The primitive ritual of
spearfishing—seen in the darkness and without sound—is juxta-
posed against the sportsmanship of "trophy fishing"—a daylight enterprise undertaken by spirited hobbyists.

The lack of a tribal spokesperson further contributes to the
film-myth narrative, evoking the caricature that Trimble (1988)
describes as "the silent Indian:"

> The wooden cigar-store Indian, as he stands alone, staring off into
> space, saying nothing, is the notion of an Indian of many Ameri-
> cans. (p. 188)

Trimble points out that the film stereotype of the Native
American "good guy" is as merely a sidekick to the white hero:
"The character is inevitably inferior to whites, but slightly
more sophisticated than other Indians" (p. 190). We never hear
from the tribal leader who sits at the news conference table;
rather, a white state official is called upon to explain the agreement. Although he appears to be in conflict with Bud Grant
and the white protestors, his argument is not one that clarifies
the Native American position, nor does it offer any historical
perspective. He simply explains that without the agreement,
the protesters stand to suffer a greater loss in the courts.

His reasoning is countered first by the images of the protestors on the Capitol Building steps, whose signs appeal to the
governor for help and show the universal "no" sign over the word
"nets." (Interestingly, KARE's journalists play up the spearfishing angle, although netting appears to be just as much a part
of the controversy.) Reporter Stauffer explains that the agreement's critics "say that Indians gave up their rights long ago
under subsequent treaties and that Minnesota would win in
court." Again, no historical perspective is provided that might
explain that Native American treaties with the U.S. government

did not so much involve Indians "giving up their rights" as having those rights taken from them.

The critics' position is further articulated by spokesman Bud Grant. Although he would not need an introduction to Minnesota viewers—he led the Vikings to three Superbowls and, years before, was a star athlete at the University of Minnesota—the "headlines" that ran before the news program had identified him. The anchor announced the agreement and explained, "We'll get reactions from the number one crusader against the plan, former Vikings coach Bud Grant." We briefly see a long shot of Grant standing at a microphone, surrounded by some of the protesters on the steps of the Capitol, smiling as he appears to be taunted by a Native American man. (Grant's smile seems to diminish the man's position, as if it is not to be taken seriously.) The "headline" sequence seems out of step with the "package" that follows. In the story, we do not see Grant with the protestors, nor do we see a Native American counterprotest. When interviewed, Grant is no longer on the steps, but seated in a room surrounded by football memorabilia. The Native American man whom we see so briefly does not appear in the story that follows.

In the story Grant is introduced as the honorary chairman of the Save Mille Lacs Association, but the Viking jerseys and helmets that hang behind him clearly link him to his status as a local hero. The long, low angle shot, in fact, seems intended to connect the former coach with his football success; he is neatly framed next to the jersey of his star quarterback, Fran Tarkenton. Grant's explanation of the group's opposition to the treaty becomes the story's commonsense understanding: "I think there is a right and a wrong." He then asks what appear to be rhetorical questions: "Why should one group of people be allowed to do something another group of people cannot do? Why should they have exclusive rights?" Without the presence of an on-camera respondent, Grant—a local legend, the voice of middle-America—dominates the story's message. Answers to his rhetorical questions would possibly go a long way in explaining the tribe's view: There are plenty of historical reasons for why "one group" should be allowed to something "another group" cannot. And there is certainly an argument for Native American "exclusive rights," although we never hear it in this story.

The marginalization of the Native American position is furthered by the reporter's response when coanchor Paul Magers asks him toward the end of the story, "Is the tribe happy with [the agreement] as well?" Stauffer replies that the tribe's negotiator, whom he describes as "their sort of commissioner of the division of natural resources, if you please," was at the news conference, and that he had supported it. Stauffer's description of the negotiator implies that the man has either no official title or a title that a white audience might not understand. He offers the white counterpart's title in explanation, his "if you please" compounding the story's sense of otherness about the tribe. Why we do not hear from a tribe member is never made clear, implying that either the Native Americans have nothing significant to add to the story or that they are incapable of articulating their position. Stauffer continues his response by explaining that the tribe will draft its own fishing regulations as part of the agreement, "which they say will be consistent with state regulations and handled responsibly," implying that the tribe might somehow handle the regulations *irresponsibly*.

The KARE journalists who contributed to the coverage likely focused on the story's controversy to add a sense of drama and attempted to balance the coverage with white explanations of the tribe's position. But the narrative's persistent marginalization of a Native American perspective feeds what Trimble (1988) says is "the prevailing image of the Indian as a dependent, helpless child" (p. 200). The journalists were simply offering their own perspective, attempting to cover the story as dutifully as possible. But their perspective is one that carries the weight of years of film and textbook stereotypes. As cultural critic bell hooks (1992) explains,

> Both African and Native Americans have been deeply affected by the degrading representations of red and black people that continue to be the dominant images projected by movies and television. Portrayed as cowardly, cannibalistic, uncivilized, the images of "Indians" mirror screen images of Africans. When most people watch degrading images of red and black people daily on television, they do not think about the way these images cause pain and grief. (p. 186)

▨ Summary

This chapter has attempted to demonstrate the perseverance of overt racism in the news. It argues that "old fashioned" and "everyday" racism persist in two ways: First, the paucity of coverage of minorities and minority life contributes to a myth of marginalization—people of color exist at the periphery of mainstream society and do not merit the attention granted to whites. Second, some news coverage—albeit infrequent—reflects traditional racist perceptions of people of color and amplifies that marginalization.

The "invisibility" of minority life in news coverage has been described in quantitative research that describes a severe short-age of minority journalists and coverage that ignores and stereotypes minority life. The newscasts viewed for this study echoed that underrepresentation. Even though the news is not entirely white, the infrequent presence of journalists of color and of minority news sources dictates an otherness that is com-pounded when the coverage that does exist perpetuates tradi-tional racist notions about minority life. As Simmons (1993) argues, "The media overwhelmingly fail to incorporate suffi-cient information about the social context or historical devel-opment of issues involving race and class" (p. 143).

That failure was evident in the two cases interpreted in this chapter. A white, commonsense understanding of the issues was reflected in the stories' words and images. It is unlikely that the white journalists who covered the events intended to marginal-ize the minority communities, and they clearly attempted to present minority viewpoints on the issues. But the stories' mythical understandings and dominant culture interpretations of race reflected the "everyday" form of racism described by Essed (1991).

One might argue that I have read too much into too little in that I found only two stories—out of about 900 reviewed for this study—that seemed to overtly perpetuate a myth of marginality about minorities. What those two stories represent, however, is a persistence of racial insensitivity that—when compounded by the news media's general underrepresentation of minority life—can contribute to a dangerous ignorance about people of color and a continuance of discrimination and injustice. And when

coupled with the more subtle forms of contemporary racism—
like those described in the next two chapters—persistence of the
traditional form becomes even more profound. As West (1993)
has observed:

> How we set up the terms for discussing racial issues shapes our
> perception and response to these issues. As long as black people
> are viewed as a "them," the burden falls on blacks to do all the
> "cultural" and "moral" work necessary for healthy race relations.
> The implication is that only certain Americans can define what it
> means to be American—and the rest must simply "fit in." (p. 3)

My cousin from Wisconsin is certainly not alone as an American who senses that the news media could be doing more to
address important concerns and the issues related to racism in
this country. A quarter of a century after it was issued, this
observation of the Kerner Commission (1968) seems as appropriate as ever:

> It is the responsibility of the news media to tell the story of race
> relations in America, and with notable exceptions, the media have
> not yet turned to the task with the wisdom, sensitivity, and expertise
> it demands. (p. 384)

▨ Notes

1. I recognize that identifying the ethnic heritage of television
journalists by simply watching the newscasts does not assure a fully
accurate assessment. In this book I will make reference to the race of
a number of journalists and people who served as on-camera sources
in stories. The identifications are based on what *appears* to be the racial
orientation of the subjects and may not be entirely precise.

2. I have intentionally not included a content analysis of the race
of news sources for this study. Those kinds of analyses have been done
elsewhere by quantitative researchers. A statistical analysis of the
roughly 900 stories viewed for this study would have reflected the
obvious—that sources seen on camera were almost always white, that
African American news sources were most likely to be seen in crime-
related or sports coverage and that Latino, Asian and Native American
news sources were virtually nonexistent.

CHAPTER 4

A Myth of Difference
RACIAL STEREOTYPES
AND THE NEWS

The subtlest and most pervasive of all influences are those which create and maintain the repertory of stereotypes. We imagine most things before we experience them. And those perceptions, unless education has made us acutely aware, govern deeply the whole process of perception. They mark out certain objects as familiar or strange, emphasizing the difference, so that the slightly familiar is seen as very familiar, and the somewhat strange as sharply alien.

—*Walter Lippmann (1922, pp. 89-90)*

. . . we make you laugh.
we sing, we dance for you.
you do not see us.
you see us
only when we wreak havoc
in your streets,
framed nightly on your tv screens,
you see us only
when we leap
out of your wildest dreams.

—*Mwatabu S. Okantah (1993, p. 139)*

A hmad Rashad, a former National Football League star who became a network sports commentator, once made this observation about the announcers who broadcast American sporting events:

> If you close your eyes and listen, you can tell whether a commentator is discussing a white or a black athlete. When he says that somebody is a "natural," so fluid and graceful, you know he's talking about a black performer. When you hear that this other guy's a hard worker, or that he comes to play every day on the strength of guts and intelligence, you know that the player in question is white. Just open your eyes. (1988, p. 83)

The announcers who make these kinds of observations probably do not consider themselves racists. In fact, they likely consider their remarks to be complimentary. But their comments reflect stereotypical thinking about African Americans that is rooted in the traditions of overt racism that dominated white American thought for hundreds of years.

Gaertner and Dovidio (1986) describe "aversive racism"—a contemporary and more subtle form of racial prejudice—in explaining the behavior of well-intentioned whites who inadvertently display racial bias. "When norms are clear," they write, "bias is unlikely to occur; when norms are ambiguous or conflicting, discrimination is often exhibited" (p. 85). In describing the athletic prowess of blacks as "natural" and of whites as the result of "hard work" and "intelligence," sports commentators exhibit an aversive racist perspective: They would like to think of athletes of all colors as equals, yet their comments show that when "norms are ambiguous or conflicting"—for example, what it is that determines athletic success—stereotypical attitudes can prevail. As Gaertner and Dovidio write, "We do not mean . . . that contemporary white Americans are hypocritical; rather, they are victims of cultural forces and cognitive processes that continue to promote prejudice and racism" (p. 85).

The local television newscasts viewed for this study occasionally included coverage that reflected similar effects of "cultural forces and cognitive processes." News organizations, even though largely made up of white journalists, most certainly attempt to offer fair and unbiased coverage, but that coverage often reflects—however subtly—a commonsense version of American society that understands ethnic minorities as "others," as different. This can be a dangerous perception. Calling for a boycott of network TV news—which he said unfairly portrayed African and Hispanic Americans—author Ismael Reed (1991) wrote in a *New York Times* column,

> The exclusion of a variety of viewpoints and the inability to respond to unbalanced stories are just as much a censorship problem as is the suppression of books and writers in other countries. (p. A25)

Local television news may be contributing to a similar kind of "censorship." By continuing to project stereotypical notions of ethnic minorities, news organizations advance racist understandings of nonwhite America. As Cornel West (1993) writes,

> To engage in a serious discussion of race in America, we must begin not with the problems of black people but with the flaws of American society—flaws rooted in historic inequalities and long-standing cultural stereotypes. (p. 3)

If the news is perpetuating those stereotypes, it could well be delaying the "serious discussion of race" that might lead to a more understanding and tolerant society.

Previous research on ethnic stereotyping in the news media (e.g., Boskin, 1980; Dates & Barlow, 1990; MacDonald, 1983; Martindale, 1986, 1990a, 1990b; Wilson & Gutiérrez, 1985) has identified the two most common news media stereotypes of African Americans. The first is the dual "negative" image of blacks, which Boskin (1980) describes this way:

> Since the institutionalization of slavery in the seventeenth century, the black person has been envisioned either as a Sambo or a savage, and these constructs developed by the majority culture have been extremely effective and long lasting. . . . By labeling and perpetuating Sambo—meaning lazy, indolent, carefree, optimistic, and intellectually limited—and the savage—a synonym for sexual

prowess, dangerousness, and impulsiveness—white society created and sustained a social and psychological distance. (p. 142)

The "savage-Sambo" stereotype, as Martindale (1990a, p. 42)
calls it, is most commonly reflected in coverage of crime.

The second stereotype is the "positive" image of blacks whose
success is acceptable only in the world of entertainment—athletes, singers, comedians, actors—in what MacDonald (1983)
calls "minstrel-show style." He asks, "Is it . . . because most
Americans, specifically nonblack Americans, find more enjoyment in such characterizations than they do in serious, penetrat-
ing images of black men and women?" (p. 236). This "positive"
stereotype, then, is hardly positive, especially when it undermines coverage which might offer a more accurate perspective
of America's minority communities.

Newscasts viewed for this study reflected the tendency of local
television news organizations to cast African Americans (as well
as members of other minority groups) in the mold of the
traditional stereotypes. The coverage reflects a mythical understanding of nonwhite Americans as different from nonminority
Americans. The purpose of this chapter is to analyze stories that
contribute to this mythology of difference in terms of their
symbolic repercussions—what messages do the stories ultimately send? First, I will look at the "positive" stereotype of
African American success in the worlds of sports and entertainment; I will discuss the frequency of coverage that portrayed
African Americans in varying roles as "entertainers" and closely
"read" two stories in terms of their propagation of stereotypes.
Second, I will discuss the frequency of the appearance of minority subjects in crime coverage and "read" several crime
stories in terms of their contributions to stereotypical notions
about Americans of color.

The "Positive" Stereotype: African Americans as Entertainers and Athletes

In the last chapter I briefly discussed the paucity of minority
subjects in stories that "localized" the events surrounding the
inauguration of President Clinton. Several stations did, however,

carry extensive coverage of a preinauguration ball; performers shown at that ball included—almost exclusively—black entertainers, among them Aretha Franklin, Chuck Berry, Little Richard, Diana Ross, Quincy Jones and Grover Washington, Jr. Considering the infrequency of coverage of African Americans in other capacities at the inauguration—as elected officials or participatory citizens—the coverage serves as one example of the media's tendency to portray minority success only in the arena of entertainment. As Hacker (1992) writes, "White America still prefers its black people to be performers who divert them as athletes and musicians and comedians" (p. 34). Perhaps coverage of the black performers was intended to "balance" the stations' coverage of the inauguration; because so few minority subjects were featured in other inauguration stories, coverage of the preinaugural ball gave stations a chance to show the ethnic diversity that many of the reporters in attendance described.

Some news executives may also feel that coverage of African American athletes helps to offset the invisibility of minorities in news programming's general coverage. Far and away the most frequent coverage of African Americans in the newscasts viewed for this study was during the sports reports. Clearly, this is a reflection of white America's acceptance—which was initially reluctant, at best—of black athletic success; it also reflects the fact that sports is one area in which African Americans have been allowed to compete on an even field. Virtually every station covered stories that included black athletes. The stories included regular interviews with African American athletes and highlighted their achievements.

What also stood out about the coverage—and which accurately depicts the state of sports in America—was the scarcity of African American coaches and managers. Because the newscasts were broadcast in the heart of the basketball season, most covered local college and high school games as well as the National Basketball Association. Although dozens of African American ballplayers were featured in the reports, few black coaches were evident. This is not a criticism of the coverage but points to evidence of the mythical thinking of many white Americans—blacks have a "natural" ability to compete as athletes but not a "natural" mentality to lead and direct teams.

A mythology of difference surfaced in other ways during the newscasts. In coverage of one sports story, for instance, we get a double dose of stereotyping. Charles Barkley, an African American basketball star in the National Basketball Association (the "positive" stereotype), is also seen as the dangerous and impulsive "savage" Boskin (1980) describes (the "negative" stereotype). Virtually every station ran the sensational footage from a January 18 game between Barkley's Phoenix Suns and the New York Knicks. As the game (a close one that the Suns lost) ended, an irate Barkley jumped over the scorer's table and chased the referees down an exit tunnel in Madison Square Garden. Cameras followed as Barkley taunted the referees. Some stations also carried excerpts from a locker room interview with Barkley that followed.

Whether the videotape of this incident merited the extensive coverage it received is immaterial; clearly, it was dramatic and made for "good television." Had a white superstar behaved in a similar manner, the story would have likely been given equal play. But given the fact that coverage of athletics constitutes the largest portion of local television news coverage of African Americans, the story carries different connotations and mythological weight.

Detroit's WDIV anchor Emery King pointed out the irony in Barkley's behavior occurring on the Martin Luther King, Jr. holiday.[1] In introducing the 11 p.m. sports report on January 18 he commented, "Well, on this holiday of peace and non-violence, we find Charles Barkley jumping over tables, going after refs and all kinds of stuff." His seemingly off-the-cuff remark serves to contrast Barkley's tirade with the station's earlier coverage of the King holiday. Whatever images we saw in the earlier coverage that may have counteracted the traditional stereotypes, we are left with a final portrait that embodies them.

The 10 p.m. newscast from Chicago's WMAQ carried the most extensive coverage of the Barkley tirade. (WMAQ declined a request for permission to reproduce a complete transcript of the story.) In the 39-second report we see Barkley missing a shot at the game's conclusion that would have tied the score. Sports anchor Mark Giangreco observes, "Looks like he got fouled, there was no call, and the Knicks beat the Suns." Next we see the tape of Barkley at the scorer's table shouting at the refs as they depart. He is restrained by a teammate, but frees himself, jumps over the table and follows the refs down the exit tunnel. Giangreco says, "Barkley went nuts" as we see Barkley talking loudly to the referees as they descend down the tunnel. Barkley, who has apparently been told by the ref that he will be fined for his actions, can be heard saying, "Don't talk about costing me money." He continues talking, but his words cannot be discerned.

Next we see a close-up of a shirtless Barkley seated at his locker surrounded by microphones. Apparently in response to a question about being fined, he says, "The league, they're making money. They don't control people with money. This is not where you can control people with money. I know you white guys would like to keep it like that. I'm just kidding. I shouldn't joke like that." Before moving on to the rest of the NBA scores, Giangreco scoldingly responds to the comments: "Charles."

Although practically all of the sportscasts on January 18 carried videotape of the incident (and all presumably had access to the same satellite feeds of the sports highlights), WMAQ was the only station to carry Barkley's final remarks. Most stations carried coverage of Barkley's leap over the scorer's table, and several also ran some of his comments from the locker room interview.

Why the stations chose not to broadcast Barkley's remarks about "you white guys" raises interesting questions. The "white guys" of whom Barkley speaks appear to be either the journalists who are surrounding him (we only see microphones) or the executives who run the NBA, perhaps both. But the "white guys" also seem to represent America's power structure, which allows successful African American athletes to become wealthy but maintains a status quo hegemony. In Barkley's words, that structure "control[s] people with money." The fact that most stations chose not to run his comments appears to reflect a sense of uneasiness about the remarks among sports journalists.

Barkley quickly backs off his comments, saying, "I'm just kidding. I shouldn't joke like that." But his reflexive reaction has already surfaced. Barkley has not always avoided commenting on racial issues during his NBA career, and in this moment we sense his apparent dissatisfaction with a society in which he is employed by wealthy white executives and surrounded by white journalists. He hedges off of his comments, perhaps sensing their controversial nature. In this moment he does seem to be "controlled" by a system in which he is valued only for his success as a basketball star, an entertainer.

WMAQ's Giangreco, who is white (like 92% of the sports anchors and reporters seen in this study—see Appendix B), seems to scold Barkley in his final comment, "Charles." His tone implies that Barkley has said something offensive or improper. Like the stations that chose not to carry the remarks, Giangreco's commonsense understanding of Barkley's words implies that Barkley is out of line and that "white guys" do not "control people with money."

The coverage of Barkley's tirade had cast him in the stereotypical role of a menacing aggressor. Giangreco says Barkley "went nuts." Other sportscasters used similar descriptions, including a Detroit announcer who said Barkley had gone "ballistic." Indeed, Barkley's behavior was unusual and probably merited the attention it received. And on this Martin Luther King, Jr. holiday, the image may have been counteracted by less stereotypical portrayals of African Americans. But considering the general invisibility of minority Americans in the news, the image of a black athlete who has lost his temper augments the dominant image and contributes to the perpetuation of traditional stereotypical notions.

This combination of the "positive" and "negative" stereotypes is not necessarily limited to sports coverage. More than once in the non-sports sections of the newscasts viewed for this study were athletics and African Americans linked in a manner that advanced similar mythological thinking. Milwaukee's WITI, for instance, carried a 2-minute story on an inner-city midnight basketball league that also evoked dual stereotypes. (WITI-TV declined a request for permission to reproduce a complete transcript of the story.)

On a denotative level, the story is a kind of "feel good" account of an urban sports program designed to make a positive contribution to the community. In his introduction, anchor Vince Gibbens says it is "aimed at getting young men from the inner-city on their feet." Reporter Phil Harris then tells us,

> The goal of the basketball league is to give 18- to 25-year-olds
> something positive to do in the late night hours. One benefit to
> the community is keeping these young men off the street and out
> of potential trouble.

He interviews the league's commissioner, who praises the participants: "One thing I do want to say is that these guys behave
like gentlemen. Not one argument, no fighting, no nothing."
One of the players says the league is fun, and that "it's just
like watching the pros, except you're in it."

The story ends in a dialogue between anchor Gibbens and
reporter Harris in which they discuss team names, uniforms
and the league's waiting list for interested players. The league's
phone number is shown on screen, which Gibbens repeats at the
end of the story. The story closes with a full shot of coanchors
Gibbens and Joyce Garbaciak seated on the news set. Gibbens
ends the story by saying, "Good idea." Garbaciak nods in agreement, offering an enthusiastic, "Uh-huh."

On a connotative level, the story seems to reveal further stereotypical understandings of African American life. As in the Barkley
story, basketball appears to be an arena in which African
American success is far more feasible than outside of it. In both
stories, basketball is seen as a means to economic independence.
Barkley's athletic accomplishments have made him wealthy,
although he may feel "controlled" by white society despite that
wealth. For the participants in the midnight basketball league,
athletics may lead to jobs, although the potential employers
described by the commissioner—"Pic-N-Save [a department
store chain] and various places"—hardly offer much hope for
financial prosperity.

The story, according to anchor Gibbens's introduction, is
about "a special program aimed at getting young men from the
inner-city on their feet." Although their race is not mentioned,
all of those who are seen on the court during the story appear
to be African Americans. His description presumes that the men
who are competing in the league are somehow "off their feet,"
and that basketball is a possible means to their recovery. Reporter
Harris adds to this commonsense understanding by explaining
the program's advantages.[2] He tells us that the league's goal is
to give the participants "something positive to do in the late

night hours." He adds, "One benefit to the community is keeping these young men off the street and out of potential trouble."
Harris's comments suggest that—without the league—the men
will have only "negative" things to do late at night; they will
be "on the street," "potential trouble." This point of view is
reinforced in the interview with the league's commissioner,
who implies a similar characterization of the players: "One
thing I do want to say is that these guys behave like gentlemen.
Not one argument, no fighting, no nothing." In what may be
an attempt to assuage a stereotypical view of the "savage"
African American men from the inner city, the commissioner's
comments simply add to WITI's mythical narrative—this is a
program that will offer hope for men who have been stereotyped as dangerous, impulsive. Clearly, the intention of the
station was not to reinforce negative stereotypes about African
American men. It could be argued, in fact, that a story like this
one actually debunks the standard mythology by focusing on
a constructive program designed to improve inner-city life. But
in the context of typical local television news coverage—coverage that generally ignores minority communities or features
people of color in a stereotypical manner—the story contributes
to a mythology of difference.

In this miniature myth, basketball replaces missionary religion as the possible salvation for the "untamed." Unquestion-
ably a popular game in America's inner cities, basketball in this
story carries more substantial meaning. Not only is it a route
out of the crime and poverty of urban life for the fortunate few
who make it to the NBA, it can also deliver the less fortunate,
the less talented. As the one player from the league who is
interviewed says, "It's just like . . . the pros, except you're in
it."

We do not find out from this story how many of the league's
160 participants actually need to "get on their feet." We do not
know how many are unemployed, or how many employers are
actually willing to hire them. No explanations are offered that
might help us understand the "potential trouble" that these
men might get into. If, indeed, these men are prone to do "negative" things, what is the reason? Although these issues are
possibly too complex to explain in a short television news
story, by neglecting them journalists contribute to a perpetu-

ation of stereotypical thinking about African American life in the inner city.

After anchor Gibbens concludes the story with, "Good idea," his commonsense perception is reinforced by his coanchor's hearty "Uh-huh." Perhaps the league is in fact a "good idea" and will contribute to a better life for its participants. But there is a good possibility that those participants are actually "on their feet," and that the program is actually not reaching many men who are truly "on the street"; those who are participating in the program may well be employed, productive members of society. But the story's mythical implications—that those participants are destined to otherwise behave negatively—contribute to the racist notions that continue to foster the poverty and despair of black urban life in America. And because the story implies that a program like the midnight basketball league could serve to combat the complex and overwhelming problems of America's cities, it dismisses the need for the kinds of shrewd and long-term programs that might actually solve those problems.

▨ The "Negative" Stereotype: Minorities as Criminals

The basketball story's mythical sense of the men as "potential trouble" is possibly based on stereotypes advanced by routine news coverage that casts nonwhite Americans in aggressive and criminal roles. The newscasts viewed for this study were pervaded with threatening images of minority crime suspects—many shown in police mug shots, others bound in handcuffs closely guarded by police. Considering the general dearth of minority coverage on the evening news, these may be the most dominant images of nonwhite Americans. As Wilson and Gutiérrez (1985) write,

> The preponderance of such reporting has led some observers to say the news media have offered an image of ethnics as "problem people," which means they are projected as people who either *have* problems or *cause* problems for society. The legacy of news exclusion thus leads to the majority audience seeing minorities as a social burden. (p. 139)

Any number of stories viewed for this study could serve to demonstrate the mythology of difference that was perpetuated in the coverage of minority criminal suspects. One typical story—about two Latino suspects in a murder at a Los Angeles pizza parlor—helps to illustrate this kind of coverage. (KNBC-TV declined a request for permission to reproduce a complete transcript of the story.)

The Los Angeles area is home to a substantial minority population. More than 37% of the population of L.A. County is Hispanic (U.S. Department of Commerce, 1990). Of the 11 KNBC journalists who appeared on camera during the 6 p.m. broadcasts January 18 and 19, only 1—field reporter Joe Rico, who filed stories both days—was Latino. This is not unusual; only about 5% of America's journalists are Hispanic, a figure that has basically held steady since the early 1980s—in contrast with the "explosive growth" of the Hispanic population of the United States (Stein, 1992, p. 22), which in 1990 was listed at about 9% (U. S. Department of Commerce). Other than a police officer who appears at a press conference on January 19, the only images of Latinos featured in stories during the two broadcasts were the police sketches of the suspects in the pizza parlor murder.

The story was run as a "reader" on KNBC's January 19, 6 p.m. broadcast. Anchor Kelly Lange's words combine with a series of images to produce the narrative. She tells us that the Los Angeles police are offering "a $25,000 reward for information on the murder of a 19-year-old pizza parlor manager, John Holden." As she reads we see a snapshot of a smiling Holden, a blond-haired white man. Lange continues, telling us that Holden was working at the restaurant the previous Thursday when "two gunmen came in and demanded money." On the screen, we see videotape of the restaurant's exterior and police milling about the crime scene. Lange, now on screen in a medium shot, tells us that Holden gave the men the money they demanded, "but they killed him anyway." She tells us that the police have released sketches of the two men, which we see. The drawing of the first suspect shows him both from the front and in profile; he wears a plain baseball cap. The second suspect is seen from the front, wearing a baseball cap that says "Cowboys." Lange reappears and concludes the story: "They are described as Hispanic, both of them about 19 or 20. One is five-foot-nine and thin, the other short with a thick mustache. If you have information call police."

The mythical nature of the narrative works around binary opposites; wholesome nonminority life is contrasted with the threatening image of the Latino suspects. Kelly Lange, an attractive blond anchorwoman, tells us of the large reward that police will pay to help catch the criminals, presumably because of the heinous nature of the crime. The snapshot in which the white victim is pictured—he is outdoors on a sunny day, standing in front of a tall shrub, handsome and smiling—underscores the cruelty of the murder; the victim was an "All-American" boy. Further driving home the theme of ruthlessness, Lange tells us that the victim cooperated with the robbers by turning over the money, but "they killed him anyway." "They" are then shown to the audience in standard police sketches. Lange identifies the men first by race, then by age and physical description. The first sketch shows the hatted suspect in the usual mug shot poses, one from the front, one in profile. The second sketch shows only the head-on shot, and we can read "Cowboys" on the top of his baseball cap. The sketches contrast with the story's white images: the smiling blond victim, the successful blond anchorwoman.

The story is typical of local television journalism's crime coverage in its identification of suspects by race, a practice that has generally fallen out of favor in the print media because of its racist implications. Television news relies on visual imagery for storytelling, even if the images may contribute to the kinds of stereotypical beliefs that advance racism and discrimination. The police sketches, like the mug shots that routinely appear on local television newscasts' crime stories, carry connotative messages of wrongdoing, of danger, of conviction-before-trial. Although they have not yet been identified, arrested or tried, the pizza parlor murderers exist as police sketches. What we know about them is very little. Other than a brief physical description, we primarily know this: "They are described as Hispanic."

The brutality of their crime is accentuated by Lange: "Two gunmen came in and demanded money. He gave it to them, but they killed him anyway." She does not reveal how she knows this; either the police or witnesses may have provided the information, but here it is a given. The narrative's emphasis is on the particular brutality of this murder. The suspects are more than just dangerous, they are ruthless, evil. The police are offering $25,000 for information. If Lange's description is accurate, this is indeed a reprehensible crime. But mixed up with the ruthlessness of the crime are the narrative's racial messages: The story is brought to you by a prominent white anchor, the voice of common sense. This was a crime committed against a happy and gainfully employed young white man. It was perpetrated by Hispanic villains, dangerous outsiders.

A cynic might wonder if the police reward would have been so substantial had the races in the situation been reversed. As Pinckney (1993) believes, "The American criminal justice system continues to maintain two standards" (p. 48)—one for whites and one for minorities. Had two white suspects brutally murdered a Latino restaurant manager, would police and media reaction to the crime have been the same? In a situation in which the races were reversed, the story's imagery would have carried different meaning. The white anchorwoman, the station's mostly white on-camera staff, the many white news sources who are routinely interviewed during the course of the news—these images could contradict any stereotypical notions of whites as dangerous and brutal people. But without similar images of Latinos in the news, we are left with no contradictory images. The police sketches and the anchor's narration become the commonsense conception of Latino America—a different place, a dangerous place.

More common in the newscasts were criminal portrayals of African Americans, often contributing to a similar mythology of difference. African Americans make up the largest minority population in the United States, accounting for about 12% of the total population (U.S. Department of Commerce, 1990). In its proclivity for coverage of urban crime, local television journalism compounds stereotypical notions about African American life. Two stories that were reported in St. Louis, MO, and Syracuse, NY, will serve to illustrate the mythological connotations carried in reports about black criminal suspects.

Of the 1.4 million people who make up the combined population of the city of St. Louis and surrounding St. Louis County, about 23% are African American (U.S. Department of Commerce,

1990). Despite the significant size of this minority population, the only African American journalist who appeared on camera during the 5 p.m. and 6 p.m. broadcasts on KSDK-TV January 18 and 19 was a reporter from a sister station in Indianapolis covering a Gary, IN, train accident. On the 6 p.m. broadcast January 19, the station covered several stories related to criminal activities, two of which involved African American male suspects, including a 2-minute "package" about a police chase that ended in the arrest of a black man. (KSDK-TV declined a request for permission to reproduce a complete transcript of the story.)

The story begins with anchor Deanne Lane's introduction: "Two policemen and a car-theft suspect were injured during a city-wide police chase earlier today. News Channel Five's Mike Owens reports the suspect tried to run over one of the injured officers." Next we see a long shot of a small crowd gathered around several police officers who surround the suspect; he is on his back on the ground with his arms spread open. That is followed by a closer shot that reveals the suspect to be a black man. Owens gives the suspect's age and tells us, "That's him, laying on the ground, surrounded by cops. He's talking even though he's been shot. He's doing more than just talking." Owens is then shown interviewing a police captain, who tells us the suspect was "smiling at the police like it was a big joke." He continues:

> He appeared to be smiling like he didn't realize what had occurred. I don't think the defendant realizes that he's going to have to stand up in court for all these offenses, assault with intent to kill a police officer, stealing an automobile and countless traffic violations.

Owens next interviews a man who witnessed part of the chase, who says, "It was a quiet afternoon, kids playing and then, boom, this happens out of nowhere." Owens then shows us the street where the chase began and where the suspect rammed a stolen car into a police car. He describes the chase, and we see a map that indicates its path. Then we're told that the chase ended in an alley, and that a police officer tackled the suspect.

We again see the suspect laying on his back on the ground with his arms spread open as police stand guard. Owens tells us that the officer who tackled the suspect as well as an officer who was struck by the stolen car sustained minor injuries, and that the suspect had been shot in the left arm. Lane concludes the story: "The 23-year-old suspect is facing charges of assaulting a police officer, car theft and leaving the scene of an accident."

The story's common sense is again that of the nonminority journalists and sources who tell it. The white anchorwoman and white reporter summarize the events; a white police captain and white witness provide the testimony. The reporter and police captain emphasize the suspect's trivialization of the situation. Reporter Owens says of the man who is being held to the ground, "He's talking even though he's been shot. He's doing more than just talking." Police Captain Jack Titone then tells us, "He was smiling at the police like it was a big joke." He repeats himself: "He appeared to be smiling like he didn't realize what had occurred. I don't think the defendant realizes that he's going to have to stand up in court for all these offenses."

The perception of the reporter and police captain—the story's interpretation of the events—is that this is a man who has committed terrible crimes but is now failing to react in the properly somber manner that would be appropriate. The man is seen as a deviant, a misfit without respect for police, for societal norms. He is not smart enough to "realize that he's going to have to stand up in court." He becomes the dual stereotype Boskin (1980) describes, a primitive "Sambo" and "savage": "carefree," "intellectually limited," "dangerous," "impulsive" (p. 142).

Martindale (1986) has observed that "American journalism's emphasis on news as events, and as controversy, helps to produce a distorted picture of race relation and of American blacks" (p. 40). In KSDK's coverage of the arrest, the station's white journalists chose to emphasize the aberrant behavior of the black suspect. The story's more general import seems questionable at best. Two police officers sustained minor injuries; a suspect was shot in the arm. The story's prominence (it was run in the first 5 minutes of that evening's program) was more likely dictated by the pictures that were available. As MacNeil (1968) once observed,

> From its inception television news has been criticized for a tendency to let pictures dictate the story. Television newsmen cannot be

blamed for wanting to put visual material on a visual medium, but when preoccupation with visual effects overrides news judgment, it encourages emphasis on action rather than on significance and the playing up of the trivial or exciting occurrences simply because they can be covered by cameras. (p. 35)

For KSDK's journalists, because the station had videotape of a deviant suspect, the story's news value likely increased. Without the tape, the story would likely have received little play or not been covered at all. But by including the coverage (and by generally omitting the black community from less stereotypical coverage), the station inadvertently accorded weight to traditional racist mythology that defines African Americans as different, as threatening, as unintelligent and immature.

The tendency of local television news to contribute to this mythology was also evident in a story covered by Syracuse's WTVH-TV on its 6 p.m. broadcast January 18. About 20% of Syracuse's 164,000 citizens are black (U.S. Department of Commerce, 1990), though all of the journalists who appeared in the 2 hours of WTVH's programming recorded for this study January 18 and 19 were white. The 6 p.m. program on January 18 included coverage of the Martin Luther King, Jr. holiday that featured interviews with several African American sources. And its sports coverage also included images of black Americans. The only other coverage that included interviews with African Americans was the program's top story, a 2-minute, 40-second "package" about a fire in which a child was killed and his mother blamed. (WTVH-TV declined a request for permission to reproduce a complete transcript of the story.)

Using questionable logic, WTVH links the fire story to a trial it had covered the previous Friday: "It has happened again," says coanchor Ron Curtis. "Central New York children left home alone, and there is a death." In the previous story, the mother had been away when the fire started. In this story, we find out that the mother was actually home when the fire occurred, and that the fire was apparently started after she had fallen asleep with a lit cigarette. But the mother is said to have left the children home alone earlier that evening, and this case is likened to the station's previous coverage of a separate fire.

So the story begins with videotaped pictures of a burned-out house and emphasis on the propounded similarity of the two fires. Coanchor Maureen Green tells us, "It was only Friday when we brought you the story of a Syracuse mother who was out drinking while fire killed her son." Curtis adds: "Then early Sunday morning another young boy died in a fire . . . and police accuse his mother of leaving him and his brother home alone." He then sends the story to a reporter: "Scott Atkinson is in the newsroom with the latest. Scotty?"

Atkinson explains: "In this case, 28-year-old Shirley Avery is accused of endangering her children by leaving them alone even though Avery was home when the fire started." He then reiterates the theme for the narrative. Ignoring the fact that she *was* home when the fire started, he asks, "When is leaving children home alone a crime?" Next we see a close-up of Victoria Dunbar, an African American woman, and Atkinson tells us, "Just Friday we brought you the story of Victoria Dunbar, who police said was out drinking while fire destroyed her apartment-home." We see pictures of another fire-damaged house, and Atkinson says, "Dunbar's 6-year-old son died in that fire which took place in Syracuse a year ago. As she left court Friday, Dunbar told us something that proved to be chillingly true."

We see another close-up of Dunbar, who says, "I'm quite sure I'm not the only parent that stays out or goes out sometimes and leaves their kids at home by themselves." (We are not told what happened at her court appearance, or if a verdict was rendered.) Atkinson then repeats the connection between the two stories by explaining that "police tell us Shirley Avery left her kids alone in the early hours Sunday while she drank at a friend's house." Police sergeant John Brennan, a white man, is shown in a close-up, telling us, "It appears she came back and again she left the house, believed to go out to find her boyfriend. She didn't return home until approximately 5 in the morning."

Atkinson then tells viewers, "Shirley Avery came home. Police suspect she fell asleep on a couch with a lighted cigarette in her hand, starting the fire." Next we see a close-up of an African American man who is identified as a neighbor of Avery. He says, "I heard the mother left them unattended. She should be held accountable for that. That's for sure." Then we see a close-up of Syracuse District Attorney Bill Fitzpatrick, who is white,

who says, "I get angry. I get angry." Atkinson explains that
the death of a child makes Fitzpatrick "particularly mad." He
adds, "Fitzpatrick tells us the presence of liquor or drugs makes
a big difference."

Seen seated at his desk, Fitzpatrick says,

> If I'm going to be able to tell a jury that—look, this is a persistent
> pattern and mom and dad didn't leave because Aunt Matilda was
> sick, they left because they wanted to go down to the local bar
> and get schnockered—then it's a much easier concept, I think, for
> a jury to understand.

Atkinson suggests that there may be some cases in which it
might be acceptable for a parent to leave a child home alone.
He says, "Fitzpatrick acknowledges that it's impossible to
come up with an absolute rule for how young is too young or
what circumstance adds up to crime." He concludes by telling
us that Avery's other sons remain hospitalized. He sends us back
to the anchors. Curtis says, "Thank you, Scotty. Scott Atkinson
reporting on yesterday's tragic fatal fire."

We never see Shirley Avery on camera, nor is her race identified in the report. But the story's racial imagery implies that she
may very well be an African American. The man who is identified as her neighbor is black, and Syracuse neighborhoods,
like those in most American cities, are largely divided on racial
lines. And the story closely links Avery with Victoria Dunbar,
the African American woman whose trial had been covered the
preceding Friday. If Avery is indeed white, no attempt is made
to establish the fact.

The story's mythology draws clear lines between races. The
whites we see include three WTVH journalists, a police captain
and the Syracuse district attorney. It is their common sense that
dictates the story's conclusions about mothers who leave their
children "home alone," a phrase Curtis uses three times in his
introduction to the story. The story's African American sources
include Victoria Dunbar, who is accused of having been out
drinking when her son died in a fire at their home, and neighbor
Patrick Steele, who comments that Avery should be held accountable for leaving her children unattended. His comment supports

the story's dominant culture understanding of the event: How could a mother leave her children home alone to die in a fire?

That understanding is hammered home in Atkinson's interview with the Syracuse district attorney, whose reaction to the incident is far more volatile than that of the African American neighbor we saw earlier. The reporter tells us that the death of a child makes Bill Fitzpatrick "particularly mad." Fitzpatrick's outrage is expressed in his use of distinctly white colloquialisms, explaining that it is easier to get convictions if juries know that the negligent parent was out drinking, "and mom and dad didn't leave because Aunt Matilda was sick, they left because they wanted to go down to the local bar and get schnockered."

Fitzpatrick's notions also stand in stark contrast to the brief comments of Victoria Dunbar, whose words are described by Atkinson as a "chillingly true" harbinger of the Avery fire: "I'm quite sure I'm not the only parent that stays out or goes out sometimes and leaves their kids at home by themselves." Her comments become the African American interpretation of the events. Dunbar's image contrasts with the white sources and journalists whose outrage at the events becomes the manifest interpretation, and the story reinforces what Wilson and Gutiérrez (1985) call "the old stereotype of ethnics as . . . too lazy to work and who indulge in drugs and sexual promiscuity" (p. 139).

That stereotype is also evoked earlier in the story when reporter Atkinson says that "Avery left her kids alone in the early hours Sunday while she drank at a friend's house," and a police source tells us she left "to go out to find her boyfriend." In describing racist sexual stereotypes, West (1993) describes the dominant culture perception of black sexuality in terms of "the exotic 'other'—closer to nature (removed from intelligence and control) and more prone to be guided by base pleasures and impulses" (p. 88).

In attempting to link the Avery fire with the court case they had covered the previous Friday, WTVH's journalists not only strain the limits of logic (had Avery *not* come home, the fire wouldn't have started) but contribute to a mythological understanding of African American life. The story's commonsense theme of outrage—reflected in the comments by the white journalists and sources—seems dictated by stereotypical thought processes that have mythologized black behavior: Look at how horrible these mothers are, out carousing instead of tending to their children. Again, the stories are based on police accounts, not completed court cases. We are not told of the results of Dunbar's trial, and Avery's trial is not likely to occur soon. But the stories implicate the guilty mothers. Their existence is seen as a disparate one from the outraged white observers. White life—displayed in the familial banter among the journalists (coanchor Curtis twice referring to reporter Scott Atkinson as "Scotty") and in Fitzpatrick's colorful verbalization of his infuriation—is hardly the same as black life.

The story's meanings are perhaps the result of local television's show business approach to the news. In efforts to build audiences, truth can sometimes be sacrificed for a "good story," and the "happy family" image of on-air journalists contributes to a singular common sense that can serve as accuser, judge and jury. As Lichter, Rothman, and Lichter (1986) observe,

> Given . . . television's need for mass audiences, and the visual and experiential information it conveys, its emphasis is bound to be on the personal and dramatic rather than the abstract and discursive. (p. 8)

The imperfections that may be inherent in the production of local television news do not only result in journalism of questionable value, but can also contribute to a distorted understanding of life outside of the majority culture.

The stories that have been discussed so far in this chapter have been included because of their representative nature; I felt they typified local television journalism's advancement of stereotypical notions about minority life. Obviously, not every story on local television news contributes to the stereotypes. But those that don't seem almost peculiar in their contradiction of the majority culture common sense that prevails. For example, a story carried by WTKR—a CBS affiliate that serves the Norfolk, VA, area—seemed to carry an oppositional understanding of African American crime. The 2-minute, 30-second "package" was carried on WTKR's 6 p.m. broadcast January 19. The story focused on the death of a young African American man who was shot outside of a party in the lobby of a local hotel.

(WTKR-TV declined a request for permission to reproduce a complete transcript of the story.)

The story is introduced by anchor Jane Gardner, who tells us that "a 25-year-old man died this morning after he was shot during a huge party." She tells us that the victim, Charlie Howerton, was known for organizing parties, then introduces reporter Patti DiVincenzo, who continues with the report from in front of the Sheraton Inn where the shooting took place. She tells us:

> Howerton was just one class short of graduating from Hampton University. He took a semester off to raise money. He had two part-time jobs and he made money organizing parties. At the Sheraton Inn party some people got out of hand and Howerton apparently thought he could handle it himself.

Next, we see a close-up of Brenda Howerton, the victim's mother. A graphic reads "angry words" as we hear her emotionally ask, "How many lives? How many young men? How many young, black men do we have to lose, shot down for no reason?" Reporter DiVincenzo then tells us that Brenda Howerton had previously worried about violence but that it hadn't touched her personally, but "now she's lost her son." We then see a close-up of a snapshot of Charlie Howerton, and DiVincenzo explains that he was shot after escorting rowdy party-goers from a party he sponsored. A Hampton police officer tells us that he was shot in the lobby of the hotel. DiVincenzo says there were witnesses to the shooting and that "Charlie's mother hopes they talk."

We see Brenda Howerton again as she says, "For anyone that's not willing to speak up, it may be their son or brother next time. And then it will be too late." We see the snapshot of Charlie Howerton again, and DiVincenzo tells us that his mother said he "was on the verge of making a difference." The close-up of Brenda Howerton cuts to a close-up of her hands, which she nervously wrings. DiVincenzo says, "Howerton is doing what she thinks Charlie would want. She's speaking out."

Howerton is nearly in tears. She says, "The answer is in us. Until we stop sitting back and waiting for somebody to do something, but we say this will not be." Before concluding the piece,

DiVincenzo says that Howerton "is upset both with the gun-man and the legal system that won't or can't stop the violence" and that "she says she's going to continue to speak out." The story ends in a dialogue between DiVincenzo and anchor Gardner, who discuss memorial services for the dead man.

This story is told in a very different manner from the standard kind of crime stories we see nightly on local TV news programs. Rather than focusing on ethnic minority suspects, this story considers the impact of the crime on the African American victim and his mother. Rather than simply reporting on the crime's details, the story raises questions about a society in which violent crime is so common. The story does not feed a mythology of difference. Here, the grieving African American mother questions America's failure to combat the problems that lead to crime and violence: "How many lives? How many young men? How many young, black men do we have to lose, shot down for no reason?"

Reporter Patti DiVincenzo's description of Charlie Howerton as a committed man who was attempting to work his way through college attests to the horror of the crime. A close-up shot of a family photograph humanizes the victim, and the close-up shots of Brenda Howerton's face and wringing hands capture her despair. She emotionally appeals to witnesses of the crime to come forward: "It may be their son or brother next time. And then it will be too late." She challenges viewers to question a system that tolerates injustice, saying, "The answer is in us. Until we stop sitting back and waiting for somebody to do something, but we say this will not be." DiVincenzo tells us that Brenda Howerton intends "to continue to speak out."

Typical local TV news coverage of this event would not have included an interview with Brenda Howerton. Rather, a police description of the crime would have sufficed. The story fails to contribute to the racial mythology of standard crime coverage. The white WTKR journalists who tell the story are not separate voices of common sense who stand apart from a nonwhite world of violence and crime. Here, they acknowledge the hope-lessness of the situation and, like the victim's mother, appear outraged by its senselessness. As DiVincenzo says as the story nears its end, "Howerton says she is upset both with the gunman and the legal system that won't or can't stop the violence." Rather

than more images of minority subjects as criminals, we see a
view of African Americans who are tragic victims of a society
that may not hold their best interests at heart. The despair of
those who are victimized by that society is a despair that all people
can understand and feel. Rather than a portrait of minority life
as different, as "other," we see that that life is not so different;
viewers of all races can identify with the sense of injustice that
is this story's essence.

▩ Summary

This chapter suggests that traditional racist stereotyping
persists in local television news coverage in the 1990s. The
stereotypes are not as blatant as their predecessors in the mass
media; rather than minstrels and Sambos, we see a more subtle
mythology about minority life—the product of majority culture stereotyping that is inadvertently communicated by TV
journalists. Those journalists would likely defend their coverage in terms of news values and objective decision making:
African Americans have gained success in the fields of entertainment and athletics and deserve the attention they receive;
crime is prevalent in minority communities, and it is the role
of news organizations to cover criminal behavior. Hall (1980)
would describe the journalists' commonsense interpretations of
the stories as the "preferred" readings, and it is very likely that
a majority of the programs' viewers would subscribe to those
interpretations. He would describe my interpretations—which
examine the stories in the context of stereotypes and myths—as
"negotiated" or "oppositional" readings. Simply to accept the
"preferred" meanings would mean to deny the possibility that
the news media can contribute to majority culture ideology.

However well intentioned they might be, journalists (and
audience members) are likely unaware of the biases and stereotypical thinking that, as Gaertner and Dovidio (1986) point out,
are deeply rooted in the "cultural forces and cognitive processes" (p. 85) of nonminority life. Notions reflected in the news
about African Americans and other minorities appear to be based
on stereotypes that, as Lippmann (1922) observed, "govern
deeply the whole process of perception" (p. 89). Stereotypes
have the power to subvert the truth, the why-things-are-the-

way-they-are, and create other meanings, other "truths." As hooks (1992) writes,

> Like fictions, [stereotypes] are created to serve as substitutions, standing in for what is real. They are there not to tell it like it is but to invite and encourage pretense. They are a fantasy, a projection onto the Other that makes them less threatening. Stereotypes abound when there is a distance. They are an invention, a pretense that one knows when the steps that would make real knowing possible cannot be taken or are not allowed. (p. 170)

Beyond the cognitive and cultural processes that can lead to stereotypical/mythical news coverage is the news-gathering process itself, which dictates on-the-spot interpretation of events and formulaic reporting. That process seems to leave little room for understanding the complexity of the problems that have led to the perpetuation of mythological "differences" between minority and white America. As scholar Lionel Barrow, Jr., argues, mainstream news organizations are "still apt to . . . condemn black crime without any consideration of its cause— white racism" (quoted in Dates & Barlow, 1990, p. 384).

Certainly not all television news stories reflect traditional stereotypical thinking. The final story analyzed in this chapter illustrates a different approach to the coverage of criminal activity that—by avoiding the trappings of the standard journalistic process—fails to reinforce stereotypical notions about African American life. But that story was unique in its perspective and hardly represents standard crime coverage on local television news. The mythology of difference that is perpetuated by news media stereotypes is most distressing when considering the lack of coverage that might counteract the stereotypes. Researchers have documented the paucity of nonstereotypical coverage of minorities in the news, and the relative invisibility of nonwhites was evident in viewing the newscasts recorded for this study. As Wilson and Gutiérrez (1985) write, "In the absence of alternative portrayals and broadened coverage, one sided portrayals . . . could easily become the reality in the minds of the audience" (pp. 41-42).

The persistence of traditional racial stereotyping is also significant when considering the more subtle journalistic representations of race that will be described in the next chapter. When combined with those contemporary notions about race, the stereotypes appear even more alarming in their potential for affecting racial prejudice and discrimination in today's America.

※ Notes

1. Although King is African American, he seems to contribute here to majority culture mythology. The presence of minority journalists in terms of nonminority meaning-making will be discussed in the next chapter.

2. Harris is African American, but his status as a reporter here seems to align him more closely with majority culture journalists than with the black ballplayers on whom he is reporting. Again, the implications and "meanings" of minority journalists in majority myth-making will be discussed in the next chapter.

CHAPTER 5

A Myth of Assimilation
"ENLIGHTENED" RACISM
AND THE NEWS

In the world of television, [America's] open and multiracial society operates within a carefully defined social, cultural and economic assumption that keeps alive the assimilationist assumptions of racial interaction.

—Herman Gray (1986, p. 232)

In the apparently enlightened welcome that white viewers extend to the Huxtables, [we end up with] a new, sophisticated form of racism. The Huxtables' success implies the failure of a majority of black people . . . who have not achieved similar professional or material success. Television, which tells us nothing about the structures behind success or failure, leaves white viewers to assume that black people who do not measure up to their television counterparts have only themselves to blame.

—Sut Jhally & Justin Lewis (1992, pp. 137-138)

The newsman actively squeezes events into categories suitable for the smooth running of the media bureaucracy as well as ideologically significant in upholding a particular world view.

—Stanley Cohen & Jock Young (1973, p. 20)

M ost Americans are quite familiar with Cliff Huxtable and his family, the characters whose lives were featured on NBC's *The Cosby Show*. Comedian Bill Cosby's hugely successful situation comedy led the television ratings wars week after week during the second half of the 1980s. That America's most popular show featured an African American cast would seem to indicate a liberal acceptance of black life and culture among the white viewers who made up a majority of the show's audience. But some critiques of the show question the positive effects the show had on race relations in the United States. Jhally and Lewis (1992), for example, think the show contributed to an "enlightened" form of racism—a contemporary attitude among whites who look at the success of a limited number of African Americans as an indication of a progressive America in which racial discrimination no longer exists. As Jhally and Lewis explain,

> The Huxtables and other black TV characters like them are exceptions to the class-bound rules of a generally racially divided society. The rules, which patently disadvantage most African Americans, suddenly are made to appear equitable and just. We are, as a nation, lulled into a false sense of equality and equal opportunity. (p. 86)

Similarly, West (1993) argues that the "conservative behaviorist" understanding of race ignores the realities of political and economic structures, choosing to "highlight the few instances in which blacks ascend to the top, as if such success is available to all blacks, regardless of circumstances" (p. 13). He writes:

> Such a vulgar rendition of Horatio Alger in blackface may serve as a source of inspiration to some—a kind of model for those already on the right track. But it cannot serve as a substitute for serious historical and social analysis of the predicaments of and prospects for all black people, especially the grossly disadvantaged ones. (p. 13)

The politically conservative attitude West describes seems to be dictating the kinds of programs seen nightly in American

homes, raising questions about the effects that prime-time network TV shows may be having on America's racial attitudes.
Gray (1986) argues that network situation comedies misrepresent African American life and contribute to racial misunderstandings:

> [Sitcoms] emphasize black Americans who have achieved middle-
> class success, confirming in the process the belief that in the context
> of the current political, economic and cultural arrangements,
> individuals, regardless of color, can achieve the American dream.
> However, these images also exist in the absence of significant change
> in the overall position of black Americans as a social group. (p. 224)

Gray contends that the programs feed "the general and dominant assimilationist view of American race relations" (p. 227);
that is, the depiction of black sitcom characters in middle- and
upper-class situations and exhibiting values and behavior associated with those classes creates a false reality about race in
America. Gray contends that the assimilationist view defines
racial interaction in the simplistic terms of prosocial values
and attitudes espoused by the white members of the middle and
upper classes while dismissing the more complex and problematic notions of racial conflict. Writes Gray,

> Also missing are black situations and viewpoints that provide
> different and competing alternatives to the dominant assimila-
> tion model. Where alternative viewpoints appear, they are frag-
> mented, momentary and eventually absorbed into the conventional
> code of problem and solutions characteristic of the genre. (p. 227)

Gray (1991) has also argued that portrayals of privileged
African Americans on prime-time fictional television can contrast with underclass life portrayed in TV's nonfictional programming. (He contrasts images from *The Cosby Show* with those
from the 1985 PBS documentary *The Vanishing Family: Crisis
in Black America*.) Nonfictional images of African Americans as
poverty-stricken welfare recipients, drug-users or criminals contribute to an understanding of underclass African Americans as
inferior to middle- and upper-class blacks—like those on prime-
time television. Gray argues that members of the underclass

may well possess the same qualities of the sitcom characters—
hard work, sacrifice, intelligence—but in reality they "lack
the options and opportunities to realize them" (p. 303). He
concludes,

> Against fictional television representations of gifted and success-
> ful individuals, members of the urban under class are deficient.
> They are unemployed, unskilled, menacing, unmotivated, ruthless,
> and irresponsible. . . . At television's preferred level of meaning,
> these assumptions—like the images they organize and legitimate—
> occupy our common sense understandings of American racial
> inequality. (p. 303)

Those "commonsense understandings" serve to augment the
notions of enlightened racism. White Americans can smugly
argue that racial prejudice and discrimination are things of the
past and point to prominent and successful African Americans
as proof. But this is mythological thinking—the myth of The
American Dream, of America as a melting pot, of racial assimilation. Minority Americans are economically, educationally,
socially and politically disadvantaged, despite the images we
see on prime-time television.

Does the imagery of local television news feed similar mythological understandings of African American life? The purpose
of this chapter is to examine the news in terms of its contribution to the assimilationist mythology that sustains enlightened
racism. First, I will examine Entman's (1990) notion of how
"modern" racism surfaces in the news; that discussion will
include considerations of American views about *class* and how
those views may affect thinking about *race*. Second, I will examine
the newscasts recorded for this study for evidence of contemporary notions about race that advance an understanding of
minority members of the underclass as inherently inferior to the
privileged African Americans who have attained social status
and financial success. Specifically, I will interpret local television news coverage of the January 18, 1993, Martin Luther
King, Jr. holiday in terms of a journalistic common sense that
is rooted in and maintains the notions of enlightened racism.

▨ "Modern" Racism, Class and the News

Entman (1990) argues that local television news coverage can contribute to a sophisticated form of contemporary racism described as "modern" (by McConahay, 1986) or "symbolic" (by Sears, 1988) racism. This form of racism has three basic characteristics: first, a general animosity among whites toward African Americans; second, a resistance to black political demands—for instance, affirmative action or hiring quotas; and third, a belief that racial discrimination is a thing of the past. Entman found the portrayal of crime on local television news to contribute to the first characteristic; that is, the menacing images of African American criminals (like those discussed in the previous chapter) contribute to a modern racist hostility toward African Americans. He also found that local television coverage "exaggerated the degree to which black politicians (as compared with white ones) practice special interest politics" (p. 342), contributing to the second characteristic of modern racism—resistance to black political demands. Finally, Entman argues that the presence of black anchors and authority figures on the news contributes to the third characteristic of modern racism, the belief that racial discrimination no longer exists.

Entman's arguments are quite reasonable. The stereotypical portrayals of people of color described in this study and elsewhere support his contention that the news media sustain menacing images of African American criminals. Entman's findings on the coverage of black politicians is supported by Martindale's (1990) study in which she identifies the black politician as a contemporary news stereotype; that is, she found an overabundance of coverage of black politicians at the expense of "a more varied and accurate picture of black Americans" (p. 49), although she found the stereotype to be a generally positive one.[1] And Entman's argument about the "meaning" of African American anchors appears to parallel the thinking of Jhally and Lewis (1992), who contend that the presence of black middle- and upper-class television characters "implies the failure of a majority of black people . . . who have not achieved similar professional or material success" (p. 137).

Entman's interpretation of the significance of black anchors also seems tenable when considering the presence of African American journalists in stories that feed traditional racist stereotypes. Two of the stories interpreted in the last chapter to contribute to those stereotypes included contributions from a black anchor and a black reporter. Coverage of Charles Barkley's tirade, for instance, was introduced by Emery King, African American anchor on Detroit's WDIV 11 p.m. newscast, who contrasted Barkley's behavior with that day's King holiday and its emphasis on peace and nonviolence. The anchor's comments inadvertently contribute to the news media stereotype of the "savage" African American. Similarly, African American reporter Phil Harris's coverage of Milwaukee's midnight basketball league also advanced stereotypical notions about African American men from the inner city.

Entman argues that the mere presence of African American anchors—economically and socially successful representatives of middle- and upper-class black America—contributes to the modern racist conception of racism as a thing of the past. But perhaps more important is their apparent acceptance of majority culture common sense, which lends credence to the news media's racial mythology. That minority journalists might adopt the hegemonic news values of overwhelmingly white, middle-class newsrooms is not surprising. Research has indicated that journalists tend to conform to the values of their news organizations as a means of socialization (Breed, 1960; Dimmick, 1974). For minority journalists, that socialization can be a perplexing matter. As journalist/author Jill Nelson (1993) argues,

> For most African American journalists, working in mainstream media entails a daily struggle with [the white, male] notion of objectivity. Each day we are required to justify ourselves, our community, and our story ideas. The more successful of us refashion ourselves in the image of white men. We go to Ivy League colleges and socialize primarily with white folks. . . .
>
> We must be emotional and professional self-censors, constantly aware that when dealing with white editors, our enthusiasm, passion, and commitment are often perceived as intimidation, anger, and lack of objectivity. Human characteristics and per-

sonality traits—such as being outspoken, stubborn, proud—are viewed as "racial," and therefore negative. (pp. 86-88)

As Gans (1979) observed, "News supports the social order of public, business, and professional, upper-middle-class, middle-aged, and white male sectors of society" (p. 61). And as Breed noted, "The cultural patterns of the newsroom produce results insufficient for wider democratic needs" (p. 194).

The "social order" Gans describes is as much about class as it is about race; America's view of its ethnic minorities is directly linked to its view of economic and social class. Jhally and Lewis (1992) think that prime-time television—with its emphasis on middle- and upper-class situations and characters—has created an understanding of members of those privileged classes as superior to members of the working and underclass; on network television's evening programming, life among the nonprivileged is generally ignored. Because most African Americans live their lives outside of the walls of the economic and social success defined by television, their stories are simply not included during prime time. With the nonprivileged out of the picture, the life of the privileged becomes TV's norm and contributes to an American perception of poor and working-class Americans as marginal, abnormal, inferior. With a majority of Americans of color living outside of the standards defined by television, they too become marginal, abnormal, inferior. Write Jhally and Lewis, "[Fictional] television, having confused people about class, becomes incomprehensible about race" (p. 135).

The news media may be contributing to similar confusion about class and race. Simmons (1993) contends that American journalists "appear unable to distinguish between race and class issues" (p. 146). He points out that many whites suffer from inadequate housing, health care and education and that the largest portion of Americans living in poverty are white. But, he writes, "The media consistently neglect to report these facts of American life" (p. 146). Mainstream journalism's common-sense notion of issues related to race and class resembles that of prime-time television programming. It marginalizes and stereotypes the lives of people who fall outside of its narrow definition of respectability. Often, this means people of color. But not always. When we see that Bill Cosby and other minority prime-time characters—as well as prominent minority TV journalists—fit nicely into the media norms, we are left with the mythical understanding that the life of privilege is equally accessible to all. As Jhally and Lewis (1992) sardonically ask, "After all, if the world is like it is on *The Cosby Show*, what is the problem?" (p. 128)

The possibility that nonwhite television journalists might be contributing to contemporary racist attitudes is certainly a perplexing matter, especially when considering the alternative of whites-only news broadcasts. But considering the arguments of prime-time television researchers and notions like enlightened racism, it seems that minority journalists may indeed be inadvertently playing a role in advancing the sophisticated attitudes of contemporary racism. Stories by journalists of all colors reflect the "preferred" meanings that Hall (1980) describes; that is, dominant newsroom values will dictate similar understandings of events by minority and nonminority newspeople.

This is especially significant when considering that the battle against racism in the news media has largely been fought in terms of minority employment. The American Society of Newspaper Editors, for instance, publishes yearly reports on minority hiring. One goal of that organization is to see that the minority population of America's newsrooms matches the general minority population of the United States. By increasing the number of minority journalists, so the thinking goes, news organizations would more fairly and accurately cover minority life. But that might not be the case, especially considering the possibility that the presence of journalists of color might not dramatically affect news coverage and could contribute to contemporary racist attitudes. But whether or not an increase in the numbers of minority journalists changes the way news gets covered, the alternatives—fewer or no minority journalists—are unacceptable. As Philadelphia columnist Linda Wright Moore (1990) argues,

> While it is likely that African Americans involved in decision making roles will adopt the news values of the white institutions for which they work, it is self-evident that, if they are *not* involved, the mix of options to be considered in making such decisions on

a day-to-day basis will be unnecessarily and perhaps irresponsibly restricted. (p. 23)

It is with this paradox in mind—that minority journalists may actually contribute to contemporary racist myths, but that that is preferred to their absence—that this chapter shall proceed. Jhally and Lewis (1992) argue that *The Cosby Show* contributed more to enlightened racist attitudes than it did to truly pluralistic understandings of race. I would contend, however, that although the presence of minority journalists may be contributing to the subtle attitudes of contemporary racism, their absence would be unacceptable and would contribute to the overtly discriminatory attitudes of the traditional racism of the past. I will, however, continue examining stories in the "negotiated/oppositional" approach described by Hall (1980); these readings are necessary in order to interpret the subtleties and nuances of contemporary racism that may be surfacing in journalistic interpretations of events. In the previous two chapters I have examined the dangers of traditional notions of racism that marginalize and stereotype people of color. In this chapter, I will consider the implications of contemporary notions of racism, keeping in mind the intricacy and sophistication of these notions.

"Enlightened" Racism and Coverage of the Martin Luther King, Jr. Holiday

Minority journalists and researchers point out that news coverage of ethnic holidays is often a less-than-serious attempt to cover minority communities; rather, it can be a cynical gesture to placate those communities. Wilson and Gutiérrez (1985), for example, argue that such coverage is often a matter of a predetermined journalistic routine:

> Stories about ethnic minorities focusing on special occasions—such as Cinco de Mayo, Chinese New Year, or Dr. Martin Luther King, Jr.'s birthday—to the exclusion of more substantive reporting is . . . indicative of policy. (p. 144)

And Greg Freeman (1991), a columnist and editor at the *St. Louis Post-Dispatch*, contends that the news media

> must begin to provide more than superficial coverage—the occasional crime story, the Martin Luther King Day events, the annual Cinco de Mayo parade, the Native American Day that comes once a year—and reach out to understand these various cultures, to cover the stories that are truly relevant to these peoples. (p. 4)

Much of the local television news coverage of the January 18, 1993 Martin Luther King, Jr., holiday may have been a superficial—even self-conscious—attempt to highlight African American communities that are generally neglected. The holiday was granted coverage on all 28 stations whose programs were recorded for this study on that date. The stories ranged from short "readers" about the various communities' events to "packages" that included contributions from several reporters and camera crews. Most of the stories reflected a sense that King's dream—of an America that does not discriminate on the basis of race—had been attained, and that the day's events represented America's triumph over its racist past. Occasionally, coverage would hint at the failure of that dream to come to fruition and acknowledge the persistence of racism in America.

The stories that would seem to fuel the notions of enlightened racism most directly were those that emphasized America's success at combatting racism. That theme was prevalent in a variety of ways. Syracuse's WTVH, for instance, acknowledged the holiday by concluding its 5:30 p.m. broadcast with a 3½ minute feature on an African American family and its members' views on King. (WTVH-TV declined a request for permission to reproduce a complete transcript of the story.)

On a denotative level, the story is a "package" covered as part of the station's recurring "Our Kids" feature. It is introduced by anchor Ron Curtis as a look "into how two generations within the same family see the man and his message." Reporter Pat Nilsen explains that many parents were alive during the civil rights era, but that "children are left to read about it in history books." She first introduces us to William Pollard, dean of the Syracuse University School of Social Work, who grew up in the pre-civil rights era South. He recalls working at a restaurant that refused service to African Americans. That recollection is followed by black and white footage of King's "I Have a Dream" speech, in which King pleads for a nation in which "my four little children will not be judged by the color of their skin but by the content of their character."

Nilsen asks, "Have things changed since [the civil rights movement]?" Pollard then relates a story in which his son Frederick's white classmate assumes that Pollard's son stole the expensive jacket that the son was wearing. The son says that "sometimes ignorance can't be helped." Nilsen next says that the recently released, Spike Lee-directed film *Malcolm X* may have made Malcolm a more popular figure than King among young African Americans. Pollard's son, William II, explains that "because of the violent ways of today's youth, they see that actions speak louder than words." But he argues that King's life demonstrates "that you can accomplish a lot of things without using your fists."

We see more of the film of King speaking as Nilsen asks, "What legacy do father and mother hope their sons will remember from Martin Luther King, Jr.?" Pollard's wife Meriette says she wants her children to "remember that they can solve conflicts peacefully." Pollard says he wants his children to have "the capacity to understand the difference between right and wrong and the courage to act to make sure the right comes to the forefront." Nilsen concludes the piece from the news desk, explaining that "the point he was making, too, Dean Pollard, with that statement, was that applies to the courage to stand up for it, with drugs, with racism, so many of our problems, and that's what we *all* want for our kids." Anchor Curtis agrees and calls the family "wonderful."

Although the story briefly acknowledges the persistence of racism, in its entirety it feeds the mythology of enlightened racism. The Pollard family is a financially and socially successful one, the father the dean of a college at a major university. American racism is largely depicted in images of the past. The nation "honors the memory" of King, and children "read about [him] in history books." His battle against racism is relegated to the black and white film-clips of another time—the white men who taunt the civil rights marchers and wave a Confederate flag represent the bigotry of an era gone-by. William Pollard recalls the injustice of the segregated South of his youth, but his present status as an esteemed academic speaks to America's triumph over that injustice.

Reporter Nilsen asks if things have changed since the days of Pollard's youth. Pollard and his son tell the story of a white boy who presumes that the son's new jacket was stolen. We are to understand that stereotypes still exist, that perhaps things haven't changed. But the anecdote fails to contradict the story's more dominant imagery of a well-adjusted and highly principled upper-middle-class African American family. As Gray (1986) argues about situation comedies that "absorb" nonassimilationist ideas "into the conventional code of problem and solutions" (p. 227), here the news coverage simultaneously admits to the persistence of racism but "absorbs" it into assimilationist ideology that contradicts it.

The Pollard family—like the fictional Huxtable family—attests to the attainability of The American Dream. Their strong sense of values is stressed and becomes the commonsense explanation of why they are different from those who are less fortunate. Pollard's older son separates himself from "the violent ways of today's youth" by identifying with King and not Malcolm X; his peers, he says, "refer more back to Malcolm" and see that "actions speak louder than words," but William Pollard II prefers King's nonviolent approach and says, "You can accomplish a lot of things without using your fists." Nilsen asks, "What legacy do father and mother hope their sons will remember from Martin Luther King, Jr.?" The mother espouses her philosophy of nonviolence; the father extols knowing the "difference between right and wrong" and having "the courage to act to make sure that the right comes to the forefront."

The family's successful assimilation into the financial and moral high ground of middle-American society is lauded by the white journalists who cover the story. Nilsen says that what the Pollards want for their kids "is what we all want for our kids"—the stressed "all" apparently meant to mean whites as well as African Americans. Curtis agrees, and adds, "Quite a family isn't it?" Their awe continues. Nilsen says, "Very, very impressive," and Curtis adds, "They're wonderful." The doting of the white journalists contributes to an understanding of the Pollards as special, as different. Their treatment of the family reinforces what Essed (1991) has described as "underestimation"; that is, their success stands out because of the apparent failure of other African American families to succeed. As she explains,

> One black who succeeds becomes salient because the invisibility of the oppressed majority is not questioned. In a social system where it is explicitly claimed that "accomplishment" is the result of "individual merit," *underestimation* is a crucial legitimization of the continuing exclusion of blacks from fair access to and use of resources. Historically the idea of white intellectual superiority has been one of the most persistent features of Euro-American ideologies on race. (p. 232)

The Pollards mythologically represent an open American society in which dreams can be fulfilled for those with the right values. They stand in stark contrast to the impoverished and criminal images of African Americans that are far more common in the news. (This story, in fact, directly proceeded WTVH's 6:00 broadcast, which lead off with the "home alone" story discussed in the previous chapter.) The Pollards are real-life Huxtables. Their success carries similar connotations to that of Bill Cosby's fictional family, which Jhally and Lewis (1992) argue implies "the failure of a majority of black people . . . who have not achieved similar professional or material success" (p. 137).

Coverage of the King holiday by New Orleans's WWL was more typical of the kind of stories local news audiences nationwide saw January 18, 1993. That station led off its 6 p.m. newscast with a 4-minute "package" that included contributions from two anchors and two reporters (see Appendix F for a complete transcript of the story). After an introduction by the coanchors, reporter Susan Roberts covered that day's downtown parade and interviewed a number of participants. We see several of shots of the marchers and hear from three unidentified men who participated. One tells us that King was "a man who was very dedicated to some very serious principles that we need to live by in order to get along." Roberts says the day "is a time for a celebration in that we can take pride in the progress, but look forward to even more unity." A second marcher says King "made contributions to society for all people, not just for black people but people of all races." A third says he is pleased with the parade's yearly growth and says he likes "the different variety of people that came out." Finally we see a segment of a speech given at a rally that concluded the march. Roberts ends the story by saying, "Organizers say it is up to people of all races to keep Dr. King's message alive, not just on this day but all year long."

Next, reporter Elizabeth Renshaw covers some of the march participants who were colleagues of King. She interviews The Reverend Simmie Harvie, who helped found the Southern Christian Leadership Conference with King in a New Orleans church. Harvie says King "had what is called a magnet. You meet him, you walk with him, he had drawing power." Renshaw then interviews another civil rights leader, Morris Jeff, Sr., who recalls King's soft-spoken manner, adding, "but what he said had meaning." We then see black and white film coverage of King's "I Have a Dream" speech and footage of white protestors at a civil rights march. (It is the same footage used in the Pollard family story.) Mr. Harvie recalls the risk of participating in the civil rights struggle. He says white opponents "were rough on us" and would attack participants as they left meeting places. We then see footage of a King speech in which he seems to sense his own martyrdom. "Longevity has its place," he says, "but I'm not concerned about that now." We see film of the balcony where he was assassinated followed by a shot of King's corpse on display. Renshaw concludes, "An assassin's bullet silenced his speech, but followers say it did not silence his message." We return to the anchors, where John Snell describes the evening's King holiday events.

Like the story on the Pollard family by Syracuse's WTVH, the New Orleans King Day coverage mythically relegates American racism to the past. In the story's second report, in fact, we see the same archival footage of angry whites jeering King and other civil rights marchers. That report, introduced with a graphic that reads "Carrying the Message," focuses on two marchers who were colleagues of King. Their memories of King and of the dangers they faced place the battle against racism in a purely historical context. The images that evoke King's assassination—including an excerpt from the speech in which he seemed to prophesy his death—are from the distant past. Reporter

Elizabeth Renshaw's commonsense conclusion to the story—
"an assassin's bullet silenced his speech, but followers say it did
not silence his message"—speaks to the triumph of King's dream.
The New Orleans's coverage feeds the same assimilationist
notions as the Syracuse coverage of the Pollards: America has
put its racist past behind it; we have plenty to celebrate.

The first report in the New Orleans coverage, titled "Celebrating a Dream," feeds similar notions of contemporary American
race relations. One marcher tell us that King's dream "lives on
and on." Although another says that "a lot of people are not
getting along the way they're supposed to," his comments are
contradicted by the story's assimilationist theme. Reporter
Susan Roberts tells us that "King's day is a time for a celebration
in part in that we can take pride in the progress, but look forward
to even more unity." One marcher says King made "contributions for all people, not just for black people but for people of
all races." Another says the march is "a real positive expression
of people remembering Martin Luther King," and he points to
"the variety of people that came out." (That "variety" seems to
be contradicted by the video coverage of the march, which
shows few—if any—nonblack participants.) Roberts concludes
her segment by saying, "The celebration is now over but the
work is not. Organizers say it is up to people of all races to keep
Dr. King's message alive, not just on this day but all year long."
Again, there is a hint at the persistence of America's racial
intolerance, but it has been contradicted by the celebratory spirit
of the coverage.

Like most of the coverage of the King holiday that was
recorded for this study, the New Orleans's stories repeatedly
refer to King's "dream" and "message." Stations in many cities
carried footage of his "I Have a Dream" speech to articulate that
message: "I have a dream that my four little children will one
day live in a nation where they will not be judged by the color
of their skin but by the content of their character." The theme
of many of the stories was one of festivity, indicating the
journalists' apparent belief in America's successful attainment
of that dream. As Roberts tells us, we can "take pride in the
progress." Certainly, King Day is a day for Americans to celebrate
the life of one of its greatest leaders. But the stations' commonsense views of harmonious race relations fail to explain the

economic and social distress that exist among so much of America's minority populations. That view seems particularly preposterous coming from a Louisiana station. Only 14 months before, white supremacist David Duke won more than 665,000 votes in his run for the state's governorship.

As in the Syracuse story, all of the journalists who contributed to the New Orleans King Day coverage were white—coanchors Snell and Angela Hill and reporters Roberts and Renshaw. But in several other cities, coverage that also contributed to assimilationist notions about race included reporting by African American journalists. WSYX in Columbus, OH, for example, sent two black reporters to cover the King holiday in that city. (WSYX declined a request for permission to reproduce a complete transcript of the story.)

The Columbus coverage, on a denotative level, was handled as a 4½ minute "package" and included a "live" report from two field reporters as well as their pretaped stories. The station's coanchors introduce the coverage, that evening's "top story." In a split-screen shot, coanchor Deborah Countiss introduces reporter Charlene Brown, who begins the coverage with a short look at the "live" entertainment at a post-march program. She explains that the boys' choir concert that we have just seen is one of a number of events planned for the evening. We then see footage of the day's march, and Brown tells us, "There are usually at least a couple of thousand people, frequently more, who join in that march, young, old, black, white, people from many different religions."

Brown says, "One thing that is significant in everything that has been happening around town is the number of kids who have participated." She then introduces reporter Tanya Hutchins, who is with her at the King Day program. Hutchins then reports on the participation of children at two of the day's events. First, we see services at a Catholic church where, according to Hutchins, "people of all races and denominations came to worship." We see city councilman Michael Coleman at the podium, saying, "When Dr. King was assassinated in 1968, he passed the torch of his dream to a new generation." Hutchins says, "And that generation was listening more intently than most would think." We hear the comments of several children about the church service and about King. Says one 10-year-old of Coleman's

address, "I learned more in that speech than I did at school."
Says another of King, "He is very special to me because he fought
for our rights so we could sit at a lunch counter and eat."

Hutchins then reports on the performances at a different
event held that day, and we see some of the rappers and dancers
who appeared earlier at a performing arts complex named for
King. Hutchins is then rejoined "live" by Brown, and she tells
her, "It was a great example, Charlene, of kids not on the streets
but actually performing and participating in activities all
throughout the city." Brown agrees, also touting the participation of young people at the day's events—"the kind of thing
you don't expect young people to do given so much of what we
cover every day and so many of the problems that we have with
our young people." The story ends with a return to a split screen
showing Brown and anchor Countiss. Countiss says, "The thing
that always comes to me on Martin Luther King Day is the fact
that the death of Dr. King really is one of the very sad chapters
in our nation's history, and yet it has been turned into a celebration of his life and everything that he stood for, and that's such
a positive thing." Brown agrees, adding, "It is a celebration of
his life, and not just a memorial to his slaying, and that gives
it a much more upbeat and—for a lot of people—much more
meaningful message."

On a connotative level, the Columbus coverage—like that in
Syracuse and New Orleans—assigns American racism to the
past. Brown describes the day's march as "very symbolic" in
that it commemorated "the marches that Dr. Martin Luther King,
Jr. himself led." The marchers "braved the cold weather to come
out and join in [honoring] . . . a peace-maker and a man that
worked for equality for all." The children who are interviewed
contribute to the story's commonsense understanding of the
struggle for racial equality as a part of American history. In
introducing the kids' remarks, reporter Hutchins says "their
generation" listened to church service speakers "more intently
than most would think," and that they "understand what
Martin Luther King was all about." One says he is "very special
to me because he fought for our rights so we could sit at a lunch
counter and eat." Another says, "He helped blacks and whites
make friends." The children's innocent failure to fully grasp the
true nature of race relations in America is understandable. But

their simplistic explanations of King's apparent triumph over racism is little different from the mythological theme espoused by the station's journalists. As coanchor Countiss remarks at the story's conclusion, "One of the very sad chapters in our nation's history . . . has been turned into a celebration."

Like the Syracuse and New Orleans stories, the Columbus coverage contains allusions to the persistence of racism, but they are overshadowed by the story's more prevalent assimilationist ideology. For instance, city councilman Michael Coleman, in his speech at the Catholic church, echoes King in saying, "We are not free until all of us are free." And in the reporters' "live" discussion of the day's events, Brown tells Hutchins that the participation of young people is "the kind of thing that you don't expect . . . given so much of what we cover every day and so many of the problems that we have with our young people." Hutchins agrees. These hints at the persistence of a society plagued with racial problems fail to contradict the story's assimilationist narrative.

Although Coleman suggests "we are not free," his status as a successful African American politician speaks to an America of equal access for all of its citizens. His polished attire may also carry a different meaning than the clothing of the black political leaders of the 1960s. As West (1993) writes,

> The black dress suits and white shirts worn by Malcolm X and Martin Luther King, Jr. signified the seriousness of their deep commitment to black freedom, whereas today the expensive tailored suits of black politicians symbolize their personal success and individual achievement. Malcolm and Martin called for the realization that black people are somebodies with which America has to reckon, whereas black politicians tend to turn our attention to *their* somebodiness owing to *their* "making it" in America. (pp. 37-38)

Similarly, the images of the African American reporters who admit to "the problems we have with our young people" confute the notion that those problems may be linked to racism. The black civic leader and journalists contribute to the mythology of enlightened racism. As Jhally and Lewis (1992) observe,

Among white people, the admission of black characters to television's upwardly mobile world gives credence to the idea that racial divisions, whether perpetuated by class barriers or racism, do not exist. Most white people are extremely receptive to such a message. (p. 135)

The story's focus on the celebratory nature of the day's events is compounded by the journalists' frequent references to the diversity of the participants. After showing us the predominantly black boys' choir, Brown says their concert is "just one of the things that's on the program." She adds,

We'll be hearing from various speakers. There will also be entertainment by a jazz group, a rock group—there's going to be a little bit of everything on the program this year.

We see two shots of the day's march. The first one, a long shot from above the marchers, does seem to show a number of white participants in the crowd. The second is a full shot of five marchers, one of whom is white. Brown describes the participants as "young, old, black, white, people from many different religions." In introducing coverage of the church service, Hutchins says, "People of all races and denominations came to worship at St. John the Evangelist Church in East Columbus." The shots of the ceremony indicate the crowd does appear to be well integrated. The assimilationist ideology continues in the children's responses to the reporter's questions. A 10-year-old African American boy says King symbolized "justice, well, for black people, standing up for black and white." A white boy says, "He helped blacks and whites make friends."

The approach of the WSYX journalists to the story suggests that the children's interpretation of race relations is an accurate one. Brown concludes the story by agreeing with Countiss's assessment of the celebratory nature of the events as "a positive thing." Says Brown,

I think that's one of the most important things to keep in mind about this celebration. It is a celebration of [King's] life, and not just a memorial to his slaying, and that gives it a much more upbeat and—for a lot of people—much more meaningful message.

Among that "lot of people" are clearly the station's journalists.
Although a celebration of the life of Dr. Martin Luther King, Jr.
is appropriate, the tone of the coverage smugly denies America's failure to attain his dream. In its words and images, it
presents a contrived understanding of racial harmony. Both
the white and black journalists contribute to the mythical
existence of the American melting pot. Perhaps most significant are the remarks made by the African American reporters
who contribute to the kind of negative stereotypes described
in the last chapter. Hutchins says the participation of young
people—and almost all of those we have seen are black—in the
days events "was a great example . . . of kids not on the streets
but actually performing and participating in activities all
throughout the city." And Brown adds that that participation
is "the kind of thing that you don't expect young people to do
given so much of what we cover every day and so many of the
problems that we have with our young people." Although the
coverage of the events could serve to counter the stereotypes,
the emphasis on their uniqueness simply compounds the
standard notions of negative behavior.

Brown's use of collective pronouns raises other questions.
Her use of the phrase "given what *we* cover every day" seems
to link her to WSYX, or perhaps to the news media in general.
And that connection seems particularly appropriate; for audience members who rely on the news media's stereotypical
images of African Americans to interpret their world, the young
people's King Day behavior is certainly not "the kind of thing
that you'd expect young people to do." But what group is
Brown aligning herself with when commenting about "the
problems that we have with our young people"? She seems now
to be aligning herself not with her fellow journalists but with
the audience. As an African American, is she commenting about
a problem in the black community? If so, she would seem to be
putting the responsibility for the problems she is referring to
solely in the hands of that community, contributing to the
enlightened racist view that white racism has nothing to do
with the economic and social injustice that pervades black
America. But her use of "we" and "us" could be aligning her
simply with Americans of all colors; in that case, she becomes
a representative of television's notion of middle-America, her

blackness a symbol of equal opportunity, her comments about the problematic nature of young people reinforcing television's mythological interpretation of race and class. Because of the station's interpretation of King Day as a celebration of America's triumph over racism, Brown's comments—however she may have intended them to be understood—directly reinforce the beliefs of enlightened racism: Prejudice and discrimination no longer exist; Americans of color who fail to achieve financial and social success have only themselves to blame.

Coverage in several other cities acknowledged the failure of King's dream to be fully realized, yet remained focused on the progress made by King and the civil rights movement. In Phoenix, for instance, where the holiday was being officially celebrated by the state of Arizona for the first time, coverage by KTVK focused on the state's delayed recognition of King Day, suggesting both the advancement of racial tolerance and the persistence of racism (see Appendix G for a complete transcript of the story).

Denotatively, that coverage was handled as a 1-minute "reader" in which coanchor Patti Kirkpatrick narrates videotape of the day's events. We see several long shots of the march as Kirkpatrick tells us that an estimated 10,000 people attended. She says, "This was truly a victory march since voters approved the statewide holiday just last November." Next we see a medium shot of Rabbi Robert Kravitz, a march participant. He says that Arizona's holiday is a "landmark" for the state and a "benchmark for the rest of the country. We voted for the holiday, and we passed it." We then see a second marcher, The Reverend Warren Stewart, who says, "It's something they should have done years ago. So it's mixed emotions: Yes, there's joy, but—hey—it's about time." Next we see several long shots of a parade in Mesa, AZ. Kirkpatrick says that it is "not a paid city holiday parade in Mesa, but many residents celebrated by holding a march for unity." She concludes, "Participants say they want people to know that King Day is not only a holiday for minorities."

KTVK's coverage hints at assimilationist mythology, but that mythology is not left entirely without contradiction. We are told that the 10,000 marchers were there "to commemorate the birthday" of King, although the marchers' chants indicate their frustration with the state's earlier votes against recognition of the day as a state holiday. Members of the crowd—seen in several long shots that indicate it is almost entirely made up of African Americans—seem to be there as much to vent their feelings of frustration as to commemorate King's birthday. "We finally got it," chants a leader. "King Day," chant members of the crowd. "Was it worth it?" he asks. "Yes," they respond. Kirkpatrick's telling of the story ignores the marchers' sense of frustration. She says the event "was truly a victory march since voters approved the statewide holiday just last November."

The assimilationist angle is supported in the use of Rabbi Kravitz—one of what is apparently only a few nonblack partici-pants—as the story's first source. He says, "What was a landmark of the state of Arizona is now a benchmark for the rest of the country. We voted for the holiday, and we passed it." Kravitz implies that Arizona's vote to approve the holiday sets a stand-ard for states whose legislatures approved the holiday without a popular vote. His comments indicate that Arizona's vote is a symbol of its racial tolerance, a model for the rest of the country. Those comments are clearly contradicted, however, by those that follow from Mr. Stewart, an African American. He says, "It's something they should have done years ago. So it's mixed emotions: Yes, there's joy, but—hey—it's about time." In his view, the day's events hardly represent the racially tolerant America that the story attempts to portray. But the coverage ends with a look at a parade in nearby Mesa, reasserting the assimilation-ist angle. The long shots of the crowd indicate a racially mixed group of marchers. Kirkpatrick tells us that the theme of that march "is a celebration of diversity," and that "participants say they want people to know that King Day is not only a holiday for minorities." That Arizona finally celebrated King Day was a story worth telling, but featuring the state as a paragon of racial harmony raises serious questions about the credibility of the coverage.

The station's coverage of the Phoenix march came nearly 10 minutes into the newscast, following a series of stories on storms and flooding that had hit the area. The weather coverage likely preempted what might have been lengthier coverage of King Day events; several stations in other parts of the country, in fact, covered the Phoenix march in more detail than did KTVK. The station's approach to the coverage—in both its brevity and its assimilationist theme—plays down the racist image of an

Arizona that had refused to enact a King holiday. As in many cities, the station included some evidence of lingering racism in its coverage, but that angle was played down.

Neither the racial makeup of the stations' on-camera journalists nor of their viewing audiences seemed to affect their approaches to coverage of King Day. For instance, several stations that covered the holiday in assimilationist fashion were in areas with substantial African American populations and utilized African American reporters. The audience for WSYX, for example, is primarily made up of Columbus's 633,000 citizens, 23% of whom are African American (U. S. Department of Commerce, 1990). And the largest portions of the New Orleans's television audience live in Orleans and Jefferson Parishes, where the population is approximately 40% black. But in Billings, MT—a city where only 7% of its population of 81,000 is nonwhite—coverage by KTVQ directly acknowledged the persistence of societal racism.

KTVQ's 4 minutes of King holiday coverage included a "live" report from reporter Jennifer Elliot as well as excerpts from an interview with a Native American representative of the Intertribal Resource Center (see Appendix H for a complete transcript of the story). The story is introduced by anchor Gus Koernig, who says, "For the first time, Americans all across the country are celebrating Martin Luther King Day." He introduces Elliot, who stands in front of a local church and tells us about the flashlight procession that will wind through Billings that evening. She then introduces Greg Krueger of the Billings Ecumenical Council. Krueger gives us more information on the march—we find out that it will pass by several churches of different denominations—and the Christian unity service that will follow.

Elliot points out that this is the 9th year of the march, but that this is the first time that it is being held in celebration of King's birthday. She asks, "Why is that different this year?" Krueger responds:

> We decided that with the rise of some different hate groups—not only worldwide but here in Billings, too—that we would join Wayman Chapel and show our support for Martin Luther King's holiday and his message of social justice and peace and tolerance.

Elliot asks if racism and "the growth of hate groups and all that here in Billings" is a bigger problem this year, and if that is "why the service is being celebrated the way it is?" Krueger says racism is "a big problem anywhere. Even if there are just a few people involved, it makes it a big problem because it is such a divisive type of thing." He points out that King's widow, Coretta Scott King, had also recently described "a resurgence of hate in our society as well as the world society." We find out that the sermon at the unity service that evening will be delivered by a Kentucky theologian who will speak on racism within religious denominations.

The coverage ends with comments by Native American leader Alda Small. Anchor Koernig introduces this segment by pointing out that "Martin Luther King's dream included *all* Americans, and the campaign for equal rights for Native Americans had its beginnings around the time King was assassinated." He says that Native American leaders in the Billings area say "change has been slow in coming, and there is still a lot of progress to be made." Next, we see Small, who says,

> If we can build just a basic understanding of one another's culture—traditions, lifestyles, family systems—I definitely believe that some of these problems with racism can be alleviated.

Koernig ends the coverage by saying that Small "hopes the new administrations in Helena and Washington will pay more attention to needs of all ethnic and racial minorities."

Although coverage in most of the cities viewed for this study—including Syracuse, New Orleans, Columbus and Phoenix—reflected a mythological understanding of King Day as a celebration of American racial tolerance, the Billings coverage directly contradicts that myth, focusing on the persistence of American racism. That Billings would employ such an approach is remarkable. Its African American population is less than 0.5%. Two white journalists steer the coverage, and a white source—Greg Krueger—expounds on the enduring racism in Billings, America and the world. The coverage also incorporates the perspective of a larger Billing's ethnic minority—Native Americans make up about 3% of its population—by interviewing a Native American leader who also points to America's failure to overcome racism.

Koernig's introduction to the story hints at that failure. By pointing out that "for the first time, Americans all across the country are celebrating Martin Luther King Day," he alludes to the fact that the state of Arizona had finally approved the day as a state holiday after highly publicized and controversial debates and votes on the issue. Reporter Elliot's questions also lead to a direct discussion of contemporary racism. She asks why the Billings Ecumenical Council had decided to celebrate the King holiday for the first time this year. Krueger, the council's representative, acknowledges that the "rise of some different hate groups" in Billings and elsewhere had motivated the group to "show our support of [King's] message of social justice and peace and tolerance."

Elliot repeats the question, asking if racism is "a bigger problem—seeing the growth of hate groups and all that here in Billings" and if that is the reason for the new approach to the service. Krueger says that racism is a "big problem anywhere. Even if there just a few people involved, it makes it a big problem because it is such a divisive type of thing." The interview is far different from what audiences saw in most other cities. Here, a white reporter and white source acknowledge and confront the persistence of racism. The two do not feed the mythology of enlightened racists who look elsewhere for reasons for the plight of American minorities.

Elliot asks about the sermon for that evening's service, and Krueger tells us that The Reverend Michael Kinnamon, a theologian and scholar from the Lexington, Kentucky Theological Seminary, will speak on racism in churches, a topic on which he is an authority. Compared to the Columbus coverage—which portrayed church life as a bastion of integration and tolerance—the Billings coverage includes religion as part of America's racist legacy.

Of the King Day stories on the 28 stations viewed for this study, the Billings coverage was the only to use a white man as its primary source. Certainly a black source was available somewhere—even in a city with so few African Americans. But KTVQ's choice to use Krueger as a spokesman against racial intolerance is an interesting one. It is possible that white audience members—particularly those who hold the subtle attitudes of contemporary racism—would find a white source who condemns racism more credible than an African American source. For the "modern" racist who believes that African Americans are overly demanding in their push for equal rights, a white man who acknowledges the persistence of racism is more difficult to refute. For the viewers of *The Cosby Show* who smugly defend their racial attitudes on the grounds that a few successful minorities prove that prejudice and discrimination do not exist, the presence of a white source who contradicts their argument may well have more impact.

But the coverage is not entirely white. Anchor Koernig's transition to the view of Native Americans includes their sense that "change has been slow in coming, and there is still a lot of progress to be made." Spokesperson Small says, "If we can build just a basic understanding of one another's culture—traditions, lifestyles, family systems—I definitely believe that some of these problems with racism can be alleviated." Koernig concludes the story with Small's view that "one way to build that understanding is providing greater ethnic representation in local and national government." The common sense of this coverage is far different from that in the many cities that chose to focus on America racial harmony. Here, the journalists and the sources they interview all seem determined to emphasize America's failure to overcome its racist legacy.

⬚ Summary

In this chapter, I have attempted to apply the findings of researchers who have examined fictional television to the non-fictional images of local television journalism. It appears that prime-time TV's messages about race and class are reinforced in coverage by local television news organizations. The interpretations of news coverage of the Dr. Martin Luther King, Jr., holiday also support Entman's (1990) findings on the existence of "modern" racism in local TV news, including the likelihood that the appearance of minority journalists may contribute to the attitudes of contemporary racists who cite the success of a limited number of African Americans in arguing that racism no longer exists in this country. This chapter further suggests that African American journalists whose reporting reflects the common sense of racial assimilation also reinforce the mythological thinking of "enlightened" racists.

The ultimate message of nearly all of the coverage of the King holiday viewed for this study was that American racism was a thing of the past. The occasional contradiction of that notion was overshadowed by the dominant theme of storytelling and imagery that testified to America as a melting pot. In its coverage of King Day, local television journalism constructed a world in which The American Dream lives, a parallel world to that of nightly network sitcoms, the world of the Huxtable family. Considering the more typical coverage of people of color on local television news—coverage that tends to marginalize and stereotype members of ethnic minorities—the existence of this other world becomes more profound. If our society is the just and fair one that was portrayed on King Day, the constant barrage of menacing images of minorities that more commonly appear on local TV news will undoubtedly fuel racist attitudes. As Jhally and Lewis (1992) write,

> Although television portrays a world of equal opportunity, most white people know that in the world at large, black people achieve less material success, on the whole, than white people. They know that black people are disproportionately likely to live in poor neighborhoods and drop out of school. How can this knowledge be reconciled with the smiling faces of the Huxtables? If we are blind to the roots of racial inequality embedded in our society's class structure, then there *is* only one way to reconcile this paradoxical state of affairs. If white people are disproportionately successful, then they must be disproportionately smarter or more willing to work hard. (p. 136)

That King Day was covered the way it was is not surprising. The social and professional processes that dictate how news is covered are based on an implicit common sense, a common sense that may have more to do with stereotyped notions about the world than with a true understanding of it. Most Americans would like to believe that their country is a tolerant and fair one, that discrimination does not exist, that equal opportunity is there for all. But what we would like to believe and what actually exists are clearly at odds. Certainly America has made strides toward King's dream, but those strides have fallen well short of the kind of racial justice that was signified in so much of the King Day reporting. The stations' superficial attempts to project racial harmony serve instead to reinforce contemporary racist notions.

That a station in Billings, MT—among the whitest places in the United States—would adopt such a different thematic approach to its coverage of the King holiday is surprising. Perhaps it was simply a matter of a small-market news organization that had not been affected by the trappings of American journalism's predetermined understanding of its world. By avoiding the standard newsroom common sense of King Day as a tribute to American racial tolerance, Billings's KTVQ contributed to a much less optimistic understanding of race relations in America. Although that understanding might be resisted by its audience, it fails to contribute to the assimilationist ideology that is at the root of enlightened racism. By avoiding commonsense, predetermined notions about race in covering the news, a news organization is more effectively playing its role as a provider of the kind of information needed for a democratically just society. As Martindale (1986) argues,

> Since the media are, by the very nature of their work, thrust into a central role in race relations, it seems only logical that they would strive to perform their jobs in such a way as to contribute toward the development of a healthier and more democratic society, rather than produce coverage that creates even more divisiveness and interracial hostility. (p. 182)

Note

1. The appearance of African American politicians in the newscasts recorded for this study was primarily limited to their appearances at Martin Luther King, Jr. holiday celebrations. It is possible that these appearances might contribute to the modern racist notion that African American politicians practice special interest politics; however, there were only a few such appearances, and it seems their more significant meaning may be in the fact that they are successful social figures whose prominence might lend credence to the belief of contemporary racists that racial discrimination no longer exists. That is an issue that will be discussed later in this chapter.

CHAPTER 6

Race, Myth and the Newspaper
HOW THE DAILY PRESS
COVERED KING DAY

Television news . . . lends a distinctive power and authority to the denigration of differences among us; it asserts that on the most fundamental level—that of deciding what is important enough to merit public attention—all Americans are essentially agreed and that wise public decisions can be reached through plebiscitarian consensus rather than through a system of institutions designed to represent and mediate differences among Americans.

—*Paul Weaver (1981, p. 292)*

Those who settle for simple answers find theirs in the portrait of America painted by the local evening news. They believe black men are sent to prison in far higher numbers than white men because black men have a far greater tendency to engage in criminal activity. The truth is more complex than that.

—*Cynthia Tucker (1994)*

Newspapers help us make sense of the blur of televised images racing by. We provide the context, the explanations, the fine print. When it comes to finding out things that government and business leaders don't want us to know, newspapers remain the last bastion of what used to be called muckraking. . . . We have tried to hold on to the basic mission in a way you rarely get from television.

—*Howard Kurtz (1994, p. 12)*

A lthough this study has focused on local television news, it does not intend to imply that it is only this form of journalism that sustains and reflects the attitudes of contemporary racism. Local TV news has certainly had its share of critics, and its penchant for attempting to increase its ratings at any cost clearly makes it easy prey. But print journalism operates out of a value system that is not that different from that which governs local TV news, especially in terms of how race and class are understood and portrayed. Headlines, stories and still photographs carried in local dailies can carry meanings not so different from the reports and videotaped pictures on the evening news.

Even America's most prominent news organizations can fall culpable to blatant racial myth-making. Anyone familiar with the fiasco that surrounded the publication of the first edition of the *Washington Post Sunday Magazine* in 1986 knows that even our nation's top journalists can commit egregious errors of judgment. The magazine was the focus of months of protests after it published a horrendous article about an African American musician accused of criminal activity, replete with (posed) terrifying photographs—including a most menacing one that filled the magazine's cover. That edition also included a columnist's support for a local retailer who refused to allow young African Americans into his shop. However inadvertently, the *Post* had reinforced the most horrid of black stereotypes. Jill Nelson (1993), an African American reporter who was working for the magazine, explains the debacle in terms of blatant insensitivity:

> The consensus among [the African American audience was] that the newspaper had commissioned and printed the two articles—both of which portray black youth (and by extension, some argue, the black community) as criminal—as an intentional slap in the face.
>
> It does not occur to them that the institution that is the *Washington Post* seldom devotes much thought to black people at all, and that the editors and managers aren't diabolical. They just screwed up. (p. 60)

I agree that the journalists who produce and report stories that feed mythical notions about race rarely, if ever, do so as part of some "intentional" or "diabolical" plot. But newsroom conventions can make it easy for journalists to "screw up." This is especially true at local television news organizations, where the predetermined notions of any of several journalists who participate in the completion of a story can have a profound effect on the way a story is told. As Epstein (1973) observed,

> The entire process of reconstructing [TV news] stories tends to fulfill preconceived expectations about how various events occur. Rather than recording the actual flow of events, news follows predetermined lines, from the developing of a story line to the photographing of selected aspects of the happening to the final editing. Since each of the participants in the process—the cameraman, sound recorder, correspondent, editor and producer—has relatively fixed ideas of what material is wanted for each type of story, the "reality" produced tends to be shaped, if not predetermined, by this web of expectations. (p. 180)

In the shuffle of the daily routine of meeting deadlines, stories are often broadcast without a good deal of thought given to the more complex framework in which those stories exist, including the historical, economic, political or sociological factors that have affected the stories. And because few local television news stories run more than 90 seconds, there is not much incentive to address those complexities.

Local TV newsrooms are certainly not involved in any kind of organized, thoughtful effort to advance American racism. Indeed, many have taken steps to address issues of cultural diversity and have been proactive in their attempts to hire journalists of color and make employees more sensitive to issues of race. But within a news process that dictates the production of short, visual stories—produced by an unwieldy mechanism that network executive Reuven Frank once called "group journalism"—sensitivity can be easily misplaced.

And local television journalists are not the only guilty parties. Even the country's most prestigious news organizations (like *The Washington Post*) can make errors of judgment that have profound implications in terms of racial mythology. The purpose of this chapter is to examine news coverage by organizations that are generally held to higher journalistic standards than local television news, specifically the daily press. Does the coverage by more "serious" news organizations differ from local TV in its portrayal of American race relations? To address this issue, I examined print coverage of the Martin Luther King, Jr. holiday in the cities whose local TV news coverage was analyzed in Chapter 5: Syracuse, New Orleans, Columbus, Phoenix and Billings.

It is with some trepidation that I attempt to compare the work of television and newspaper journalists. One of the earliest studies to do so (Lyle & Wilcox, 1963) noted that such a comparison "raises the question of comparing disparate entities, of sheep to goats" (p. 158). That study included this observations, which remains as true as when originally delivered: "Overall, the *most* detailed of television stories roughly compares to the *least* detailed of newspaper stories" (p. 163). The issue here, however, is not so much the considerable difference in how the news is covered but in how the differences between the two affect the myth-making capacities of each.

▒ *Syracuse Herald-Journal* and *The Post-Standard*

Although the most extensive coverage of the King holiday by local television news organizations amounted to less than 4 minutes of coverage (usually much less), newspaper coverage generally included detailed national and local coverage, related "side-bar" stories as well as editorial and columnist commentary. In Syracuse, for example, the 5:30 broadcast included the 3½ minute feature on the Pollard family that was discussed in the previous chapter. This was among the longest stories viewed for this study to be included as part of a station's King holiday coverage. But in that city's daily newspapers, the *Syracuse Herald-Journal* and *The Post-Standard*, coverage on January 18 and 19 included several news stories written by staff reporters—ranging in length from about 600 words to nearly 2,000— as well as wire service coverage of national commemorations and a local columnist's reflections on the day's celebration. Stories written by *Herald-Journal* and *Post-Standard* reporters included (a) coverage of appearances in Syracuse by a Harvard University professor who had worked with King during the civil rights movement, (b) several stories about other local ceremonies honoring King, (c) an extensive story about school integration that focused on a school named for King, and (d) columnist Saundra Smokes's views, entitled "A Challenge for Whites to Consider."

Herald-Journal coverage included some of the similar assimilationist mythology that was so evident in the television news coverage viewed for this study. A January 18 story carried on the front page of the Metro section that focused on a visit to Syracuse by Charles V. Willie, a Harvard sociologist who had gone to college with King, ran under a headline reading, "King's Legacy: A Changed World." Like much of the local TV news coverage, the story relegated American racism to a bygone era of segregated public services and bus boycotts. But the story concluded with Willie's feelings about the state of racism in 1990s America:

> Willie told [audience members at a church service] the tradition of the "suffering servant" is as alive today as it was in 1968.
>
> "A good person can still be vilified, can still be crucified," he said. There is still much work for them to do. And he said it is useless to remember someone such as King without addressing the conditions which brought about his death: injustice, hatred, racism and segregation. These, too, remain, he said. (Reilly, 1993a, p. B1)

The following day's coverage of Willie's King Day appearance at a community center also focused on present-day racism. That story's lead included questions raised by those in attendance:

> Has King's dream been fulfilled? Why do young black men wear X on their hats instead of MLK? Why does racism persist? Is there a deeper meaning to the Los Angeles riots? (Reilly, 1993b, p. B1)

That story says that Willie's message at each of his appearances in Syracuse was consistent. He spoke about the need for building community, about the essential vitality of diversity, about how much white people need black people and vice versa, about how no group can make it on its own. He invoked King's "principle of asymmetry," which says the only way to overcome evil is with its opposite— "brutality only gives rise to more brutality . . . love is asymmetrical to hate"—and King's insistence that oppressed people must never cooperate in their own oppression. (Reilly, 1993b, p. B1)

In an appearance at Syracuse University, Willie is reported to have urged students to risk poor grades by standing up to racially abusive teachers and to push for greater diversity in the university's faculty and student body.

Though much of the local TV coverage of King Day included references to the persistence of racism in America, those references tended to be lost in the dominant theme of America's victory over racism. The *Herald-Journal*'s coverage of Charles Willie's visit to Syracuse, however, was dominated by Willie's view that American race relations had become anything but the harmonious world of which King dreamed. That view was also reflected in *Post-Standard* columnist Saundra Smokes's January 18 article. Smokes, an African American, addresses her column to white people, but

not all white people. Not the ones who write or call me to tell me why "my people," all 20 million of us, are lazy, ignorant, thieving, lying, cheating, whiny worthless drains on white society. . . .

I address my words to the white people whose minds are wide open or at least the door is cracked enough to let some other views in.

I ask you to stop sympathizing, to stop shaking your head, to stop expressing shock and dismay about prejudice, about racist acts, about the state of race relations in this country. (1993, p. E1)

Smokes writes that she is troubled that "there are so many well-intentioned whites who think they have taken a step toward ending bigotry by declaring they are liberals." She reflects on the days of the civil rights movement, when some whites marched with King and worked in their communities to battle racism. She concludes that those whites

confronted their own attitudes and contributions in this nation. They acted—at a time when it took far more courage to stand up to bigots.
  It's 1993.
  What can white people do?
  Something.

Perhaps more than any other difference between television and newspaper news is the newspaper's capability to carry analysis, including some of a very personal nature. The voice of an African American columnist can add a remarkable layer of insight to the events of the day. Few local television news organizations carry any kind of commentary these days; if they do it comes very briefly from a station manager or, occasionally, in a viewer's response to an opinion by that station manager. But there is no local television counterpart for the daily newspaper columnist, and so a level of interpretation that could go a long way in debunking standard newsroom and societal mythology does not exist.

That analytical capacity of newspaper coverage is not limited to its opinion columns. Print stories are not limited by the time restrictions that severely confine TV news coverage; they can delve more deeply into complex issues. *The Post-Standard*, for instance, carried a front-page story that ran more than 2,000 words on January 18. It was headlined "Reality Defers King's Dream." The story observed, as a sub-headline explained, "25 years after the civil rights leader's death, his vision of full integration eludes the school that bears his name."

The story examines a number of complex issues regarding the issue of school integration. First, it points out that the Syracuse plan to desegregate its public schools had—at least at one school—failed. The story begins by describing a celebration of King day at the Martin Luther King Jr. Community School:

> . . . As the students marched and sang, it was clear that one aspect of King's dream was missing. In a school district where half the children are white, nearly nine out of 10 of the children who packed Dr. King's auditorium Friday were not.
>
> Twenty-five years after the civil rights leader's death, the school named after him remains an exception to the city's generally successful integration program. (Riede, 1993, p. A1)

But the story did not pursue that angle. School integration has largely failed in most American cities—many whites fled to the suburbs or sent their children to private schools, derailing the intent of court mandates to integrate schools to assure that students of all races were given equal opportunities. At the King school, however, the school's failure to become integrated did not preclude its attempts to provide quality education. As the story tells us, "For some educators, parents and community leaders, school integration—as an end in itself—is not the vital issue it once was." The school district superintendent is quoted as saying, "We recognize that minority enrollment is high, but we also see students who are coming out of that school with incredible academic skills and ability."

The story challenges the "prevailing view," which is "acknowledged by national research" that "black students perform better when they learn alongside white students." An Urban League executive explains that students "might be better off attending a well-funded neighborhood school like Dr. King than being bused into 'a hostile community that doesn't want them.' "

The story also addresses other current issues related to education in minority communities, including Afrocentric curricula in schools predominantly attended by African American students as well as the reluctance of whites to send students to a predominantly black school like Dr. King. One white parent whose child attends the school calls it "the best-kept secret in Syracuse," adding, "I don't believe many parents understand what's happening within those walls."

For a local television news organization to tell a similar story—replete with an examination of complicated factors regarding race and education—is unfathomable. The story resists "commonsense" thinking about school integration and provides readers with information that might challenge their notions about race. Because print journalism is afforded the "luxury" of depth in its reporting, it can—at least in some instances—provide a discussion that questions standard racial mythologies.

The Phoenix Gazette

Coverage of the King holiday by *The Phoenix Gazette*, although very brief compared to newspaper coverage in Syracuse, also served to contradict the celebratory theme of stories carried by Phoenix's KTVK-TV. On January 17, the day preceding King Day, *The Phoenix Gazette* carried a page-2 story from the *Chicago Tribune* that directly questioned Arizona's justification for festive celebration of the holiday. That story began,

> Not even the hallelujahs belted out by the Baptist chorus in the America West Arena on Friday could drown out the murmurs of ambivalence marking Arizona's first full-fledged celebration of the Martin Luther King Jr. holiday. (Dellios, 1993, p. A2)

The article observed that it would be "hard to find anyone in Arizona . . . who would declare the hard-earned King/Civil Rights Day an unqualified victory." An African American woman is quoted, citing the persistence of racism in Arizona: "We've gone 20 steps forward, and 21 backward. We still have a long way to go." The article continues: "Ask any of the state's African Americans what the King holiday means, and their joy is tempered with tales of still being discriminated against by employers and snubbed by waiters."

The day after the holiday, an article that ran on page 1 of the *Gazette*'s Metro section carried this lead:

> Sen. Sandra Kennedy, D-south Phoenix, thanked Arizona for Monday's Martin Luther King holiday but said, "We are still plagued with racism." (McCloy, 1993, p. B1)

The article extensively quotes Kennedy's attacks on Arizona's tolerance of racist behavior. "The gains that we have made are slowly but surely slipping away from us," she is quoted as saying. "I feel as though I should shout from the mountaintops and valleys, 'Don't you see what's happening? Don't let history repeat itself.'"

The Phoenix Gazette's coverage of King Day, although not as extensive as that of newspapers in Syracuse, stands in stark contrast to KTVK-TV's understanding of the day as a time for Arizonans to celebrate an end to American racism. In other cities, however, that theme carried over into newspaper coverage of the holiday.

▧ *The Columbus Dispatch*

The headline at the top of the January 19, 1993 edition of *The Columbus Dispatch* reads, "King's Quest Filled With 'Love, Logic.' " A subhead reads, "Thousands in Columbus Salute Mission of Martyr." The lead identifies King as "the man honored yesterday for leading the nation toward racial equality" (Hambrick, 1993, A1). The keynote speaker, an attorney for the NAACP, is identified as the first black woman to receive a law degree from the University of Virginia, in 1970. She is quoted as saying that King " 'through love and logic' unified the country." The story tells us that a citywide celebration attracted thousands, and that a rabbi delivered the invocation at one event.

Like the coverage by Columbus' WSYX-TV, the *Dispatch* covered King Day as a celebration of American diversity: King is viewed as the man who put an end to racial discrimination. Victims of that discrimination are portrayed as survivors who have won positions of prestige and power. Americans of all races and creeds celebrate the day as equals. In its coverage, the *Dispatch* chose to highlight the celebratory aspects of King Day; certainly, the celebration merits coverage. But the story's theme, which emphasizes the attainment of King's dream, tends to raise questions about its accuracy.

The story does stray from that theme when it quotes Elaine Jones, the NAACP attorney, saying,

> "an overwhelming number" of blacks "don't even have a foot on the bottom rung" of the ladder leading to King's dream of equality and justice. She said issues facing black America today are not as clear-cut as those of the past. (Hambrick, 1993, p. A1)

Like much of the local TV news coverage of the holiday, the story only hints at a persistence of American racism; that hint is largely consumed by the coverage's general theme of racial tolerance in 1990s America.

▧ *The Times-Picayune*

Coverage in New Orleans by *The Times-Picayune* also included mixed messages about the day's celebration. Its front page on

January 19 carried a wire service story about President Bill Clinton's observation of the day as well as a story—accompanied by two photographs—about King Day celebrations in New Orleans. The Clinton story included the president's vow to learn from King in ascending "the mountaintop of American democracy" (Raum, 1993, p. A1). Later in the story, Clinton cites his election as evidence of the triumph of King's vision of American democracy:

> Clinton paid solemn tribute to King, on the holiday celebrating his birthdate, in a speech at Howard University. . . .
> "Two sons of the South are about to assume the mountaintop of American democracy, a president from a small town in Arkansas, a vice president from the hills of Tennessee, both believers in the dream and the obligations that Martin Luther King spoke," Clinton said.

The Times-Picayune's local coverage focused on the size and revelry of the crowd that marched through the city on King Day. A front-page story was accompanied by a large photograph of a man and his young son who are viewing the parade. A headline above the photo reads "Living Memory." The photo is dominated by the child's face and the man's T-shirt, which shows a picture of King next to the words "He Died to Make Me Free." The accompanying story reads,

> Drums sounded for miles along St. Claude Avenue Monday, summoning thousands into the street in celebration of what would have been the 64th birthday of the civil rights leader, the Rev. Martin Luther King, Jr. (Bell, 1993, p. A1)

It continues by describing the march, which featured public school marching bands and city officials. We are told that "people from across the metropolitan area turned out for several commemorative events," and that the mayor of New Orleans told the audience at a rally that "more than 100,000 people had come to watch the long march."

The celebratory theme of the story, however, shifts as several speakers at the rally call for an end to racial injustice. One criticizes the school system for imbalances within the schools, saying,

> There's no reason why the children of Carver (High School) should have water (leaking) in the classroom while children at Ben Franklin (High School) live in luxury. . . .
> We done lost the mission of the cotton fields. . . . We forgot that the blood of our ancestors dictates that we have to fight for the things they never saw. (Bell, 1993, p. A5)

The story quotes an observer of the rally, identified as an unemployed carpenter, who says he is

> glad "in a way" that King isn't here to see what American cities are becoming.
> "I know when he died he was talking about a war on poverty; I remember that. . . . Well, he would have lost that one. This country's about one thing: them that got shall get, and those that have not shall lose. It's a good day, pretty outside and everybody feels nice. But tomorrow's gonna be another thing." (Bell, 1993, p. A5)

Other *Times-Picayune* coverage related to the holiday also focused more on the persistence of racism than on the celebration of its demise. A page 2 wire service story about acknowledgment of the day around the United States focused on a speech by King's daughter, Bernice, who pleads with newly elected President Clinton to honor his election promises about equality and justice. She is quoted from an appearance in Atlanta, where she tells the audience,

> Let's face it, there are some people in power who have no intention of making my dad's dream a reality.
> Many here in America are merely paying lip service to the memory of Martin Luther King, Jr. (Watts, 1993, p. A2)

The Times-Picayune also included syndicated columnist Cynthia Tucker's analysis of the King celebration in its January 18 op-ed section. Tucker attacks racism within the American criminal justice system in her commemoration of King. She writes:

Those who labor to keep alive the hopes and dreams of the late Martin Luther King Jr. have an annual ritual, timed to coincide with the celebration of his birthday in January. Assessing America's progress in ameliorating the legacy of racism they sum up the State of the Dream.

I wonder where Dr. King would turn his eloquent rhetoric and uncommon courage were he alive today. I cannot help but think he would keep a sharp eye focused on a not-so-subtle pattern eating away at the foundations of black life in America: the high rate of incarceration of African American men. (Tucker, 1993, p. B5)

Tucker cites a number of statistics in arguing that the American criminal system is racist, citing one analysis that showed that "black men made up 38 percent of those arrested for drug violations," but "blacks make up only 12 percent of those who regularly use drugs." She writes,

Why the difference? Racial distinctions show themselves in many ways. Since many black Americans tend to be poor, they do not have access to the private drug treatment that is available to those who have health insurance. Their drug addictions may tend to be more visible.

She also points out that white prisoners are twice as likely as black prisoners to be given probation rather than jail-time, and that "penalties associated with crack cocaine, used mostly by blacks and Hispanics, can be 100 times worse than the penalties for powdered cocaine." She concludes by arguing that the high incarceration rate for black men "cast[s] them forever to the fringes of American society." She writes:

They will always wear the label "ex-con," they will never land steady jobs, they will hardly be able to provide for families. This does not merely defer the dream for black Americans. It endangers the dream for all.

Tucker's analysis—as well as much of the news coverage by *The Times-Picayune*—certainly undermines any "commonsense" portrayals of the celebration of King Day as a tribute to American equality and justice. Again, the voice of an African American commentator adds depth to coverage that might have ignored a more accurate and complex understanding of American race relations. The capacity of newspapers to examine complicated issues with broad and analytical coverage certainly gives the medium an advantage in addressing something as sophisticated as contemporary American racism. But not all newspapers will choose to utilize that advantage in advancing the discussion.

The Billings Gazette

The Billings Gazette's brief coverage of King Day (which included only one story, on page 1 of the City/State section) adopted the theme that dominated King Day coverage by local TV news organizations. The story begins,

> People representing several religions and races marched through downtown Billings Monday night and later packed into a city church to celebrate the birth and beliefs of civil rights leader Martin Luther King, Jr. (Ehli, 1993, p. B1)

The story says the event's organizers say that "King's teachings have not been forgotten in Billings." It quotes Greg Krueger (the same source interviewed by Billings' KTVQ-TV), saying,

> There are hate groups in Billings, but so far, they are small. We need to show that there are 10 times as many people in this city who don't think like they do. (Ehli, 1993, p. B1)

Ironically, the Billings' newspaper coverage of the event contrasts with KTVQ's. Although the Billings TV station was the only one viewed for this study that declined to adopt a common sense about the day's events that focused on the unbridled success of America's civil rights movement, *The Billings Gazette*'s brief coverage embraced that theme unequivocally.

▨ Summary

The American daily newspaper certainly has the potential to contribute to contemporary racial mythology. A number of recent studies (e.g., Gist, 1990; Martindale, 1990a, 1990b; Pease, 1988) cite problems with newspaper coverage that stereotypes and ignores Americans of color. Criminal activity is portrayed as the endeavor of choice among African Americans, while everyday life outside of the white community is largely invisible.

Employment statistics are also bothersome: Newspapers remain almost exclusively controlled by white, male executives; African American and other minority journalists make up less than 8% of the workforce on the daily press, and half of America's dailies employ only white journalists (ASNE, 1992).

Journalistic common sense—when dictated in overwhelmingly white newsrooms—makes plausible the notions about race that contribute to mythical understandings. In terms of how King Day was covered, that meant some newspapers chose to ignore the persistence of racism and highlight events that appeared to celebrate America's victory in the war against it. That was certainly the tone of the local TV news coverage viewed for this study; some of the newspaper coverage adopted that tone. As Weaver (1981) has observed,

> Many of the vices and virtues that people attribute to television or newspapers are in fact not unique to the medium in question but are instead characteristics of news as such. (p. 279)

However, the nature of the newspaper medium makes it less handy as a tool of myth-making. Because it can carry lengthy, detailed stories, it can undermine the myths that are easily bolstered by brief coverage—the theme of which can be predetermined by newsroom common sense. The capacity for more detailed reporting also allows newspapers to approach news from less routine perspectives. Much of the crime coverage in American newspapers has shifted from police-directed narrative to the perceptions of primary sources: crime victims and their families, friends and eyewitnesses.

Some newspapers have also taken on ambitious "race pro-
jects" in which integrated teams of reporters and editors examine issues related to racism. The *Akron Beacon-Journal* won a
Pulitzer Prize for its extensive series on race, titled "Coming
Together," in 1993. And *The Times-Picayune* received numerous
awards for its ambitious series, "Together Apart," which ran
for several months and covered even the most subtle kinds of
racial issues peculiar to New Orleans. It is difficult to imagine
a local television news organization considering such a project.
Daily newspapers that choose to utilize their capacity to examine such issues in depth seize what is their most valuable asset.

A second feature of newspapers that allows them to counter
the predetermined notions about race reflected in some coverage is their inclusion of commentary. Opinions by local and
national columnists, staff editorials and even letters from readers can inject a diversity of viewpoints that can be missed in
routine news coverage. Although the commentary sections in
most newspapers amount to only a tiny portion of their total
coverage, those sections serve an important function in providing differing interpretations on the events of the day, a function
that is generally dismissed by local TV news organizations.

This is unfortunate when considering that most Americans
rely on local television journalists to provide them with information about the day's events. The interpretations of those events—
usually very brief and usually relying on something visual to
tell the story—reflect a common sense (which many journalists
would describe as "objectivity") that can be immersed in racial
mythology. But newspapers hardly offer an entirely different
view of the world that could deflate local TV news mythology.
Readers do not read every word published in a newspaper. Many
simply skim headlines, and others may ignore commentary that
appears to contradict their own worldviews. In this case, the
newspaper's myth-making capacity is very much like that of
local television news.

Washington Post media critic Howard Kurtz (1994), who
condemns the press for its failure to cover America's inner cities
adequately, has challenged the newspaper industry to find a
way to get readers beyond the headlines and into the real substance of the issues of the day. Newspaper journalists "console
ourselves with high-minded claptrap about our responsibility

to inform the masses," he writes, "forgetting that you can't teach people a thing until you get them inside the tent" (p. 12). The contemporary challenge for all forms of American journalism is first to attract an audience and then have something—something of use, of substance, of truth—to say to that audience.

That the daily press—a more highly regarded form of journalism than the local TV news—would contribute less to misunderstandings of race probably has more to do with the peculiar nature of local TV news than with the quality of the journalism. Middle-American common sense about race—well entrenched in the executive offices of American news organizations (not to mention corporate America)—can dictate the tone of coverage that keeps alive America's racial mythology. Daily newspapers are just as apt to approach race from the same predetermined notions that are reflected in local TV news coverage. But this more "legitimate" source of news has the capacity to include analysis and commentary that can counter those notions. Local television news programs do not.

CHAPTER 7

Conclusion

The most striking aspect of watching and rewatching the newscasts recorded for this study—nearly 40 hours worth from 29 American cities—was the *sameness* of the programs. The local evening news in Fargo, ND, is very much like that in Dayton, OH, or in Lafayette, LA, or in Phoenix, AZ, or in New York, NY. News sets are remarkably similar (though the skylines in the background vary), and many go by similar names —Action News, Eyewitness News, News Center 5 (or 6 or 7, etc.). The anchors and reporters don the latest TV journalist fashions and wear their hair in the proper coifs of the day. On camera, they appear to be best pals with their coworkers. The vast majority of their voices are free of accents and dialects, as if they all came from the same mythical middle-American town.

The news they carry is also similar: a few minutes of hard news to start things out; if there is videotape of a fire in the area, that will lead things off. (If the fire was someplace else, it gets carried later in the newscast.) Pictures of crime suspects are granted much prominence; the severity of the crime doesn't much matter. Following the "hard" news, most stations insert a few minutes of local weather information before cutting away to the first commercial. Next we get a little more news, more weather and the sports report. Many stations also carry "news you can use" features—health or finance related stories—and whatever human interest reports are available: injured dogs or ducks, heroic deeds, amusing anecdotes. Then we get more weather.

But this study is not a critique of the homogenization of local television journalism. It is, however, interested in the *sameness* of the racial mythology that is embedded in broadcasts across the United States, and that sameness has very much to do with the homogeneous practices of local television news organizations. Those practices appear to represent a hegemonic consensus about race and class that sustains myths about life outside of white, "mainstream" America. And those myths may well be contributing to contemporary notions about race that will preclude the kind of understanding that is necessary to attain the tolerance and compassion that must precede the elimination of racial prejudice and discrimination in the United States.

When the local news ignores life outside of middle-American/ dominant culture parameters, it contributes to an understanding of minority cultures as less significant, as marginal. When journalists attempt to cover life in minority communities but neglect and dismiss the attitudes and perceptions of people of color, they compound that sense of marginality. When the news sustains stereotypical notions about nonwhite Americans as less-than-human, as immature, as savages, as derelicts, it feeds an understanding of minorities as different, as "other," as dangerous. It feeds that same understanding by exclusively highlighting the successes of African Americans in terms of sports and entertainment. The myths that for hundreds of years have governed how white Americans think about people of color must be carefully reexamined and eliminated if the news media are to play their proper societal role of providing a democratic citizenry with the kind of information it needs to act in its own best interests.

Perhaps the most dangerous myth about American life is that which ignores the very existence of racism. Journalists (of all colors) whose reporting reflects the notion that racial prejudice and discrimination do not factor into the disheartening social, political, educational and economic conditions faced by so many nonwhite Americans contribute to an assimilationist under-

standing of those conditions. That is, when news organizations—however well intentioned—implicitly accent the values
and determination of socially and economically successful minority Americans, they feed the mythological notion that that
success is equally accessible to all. So when the majority of news
accounts of people of color show them to be anything but socially
and economically successful—killers of pizza parlor employees,
mothers who leave their children home alone to die in fires, and
so on—the implication is that those people had the same options
and preparation necessary to seize The American Dream yet
chose a life of savagery and/or destitution instead. The color of
their skin becomes the implied explanation for their choice.

Local television journalism is not alone in its propagation of
contemporary racial mythology. Prime-time television and other
artifacts of popular culture reflect similar "commonsense" understandings of American race relations. Even the most prestigious news organizations are culpable, including highly regarded
daily newspapers. The process of covering the news by the daily
press—from the selection of story ideas to the reportorial routine—is not so different than that which governs local TV news.
Although newspapers can augment their coverage with more
analytical stories and opinion pieces, their front-page headlines
and photographs can carry significant mythological weight.

But the very nature of local television news makes it ideally
suited for the enhancement and manufacture of America's
myths. Local newscasts draw large audiences, the largest of any
form of journalism. The stories are told in short sound bites,
accompanied by powerful videotaped images. Words and pictures are selected to provide audience members with uncompli-
cated explanations of the events of the day, despite the unre-
ported intricacies that might complicate those explanations.

Most American news organizations are likely pleased with
their efforts to cover life in minority communities. Most journalists would likely claim to be sensitive to how they portray
people of color and how they cover life outside of the privileged
world in which they live their own lives. Many news executives
brag of their efforts to increase minority hiring. In fact, most
of the emphasis in improving coverage of minority America has
been on increasing the hiring of nonwhite journalists. Although
this is certainly a sensible approach and has undoubtedly

improved the way people of color are covered in the news, it will not—at least not in the near future—affect a change in the dominant culture understandings that determine how most stories are covered. A change in those understandings would require a massive change in mainstream American thought—an event not likely to come any time soon.

Most members of local television news audiences would "read" the news differently than I have in this study. The journalistic common sense that dictates how events are to be covered is part of a larger common sense that governs dominant culture (mostly white, mostly middle class) understandings. The news is largely covered and consumed in the preferred interpretations of that culture. But not entirely. Some journalists and some audience members resist a "common" sense that fails to acknowledge other readings of events, other interpretations.

This study—like any interpretive study—is subject to similar criticism. My reading of the news can hardly lay claim to manifest "truths" about American journalism's understanding of race and race relations. The news, like other cultural artifacts, lends itself to multiple interpretations and understandings. Should anyone else choose to sit through repeated viewings of the newscasts that I viewed for this study, their interpretations would certainly differ. The search for meaning is hardly an exact science. But I would welcome those interpretations (or any other analysis of what the media may be telling us about race in America) as part of an ongoing discussion of how the news contributes to and generates myths about American life and how it constructs "reality."

Additional interpretations of contemporary American culture that address the issues of race and class would seem especially important considering the significance of these issues in 1990s America. The capability of constructing and maintaining meanings is hardly limited to journalism. This study has examined television journalism and made repeated references to primetime television programs, but other forms of popular culture—advertising, film, music, and so on—have similar meaning-making capacities. Mass communications researchers would do well to investigate and interpret those meanings in terms of the sometimes-subtle notions of contemporary racism.

In fact, it is possible that the racial mythology reflected in the news might already be being contradicted by other forms of mass media. Media critic Jon Katz (1992) argues that young Americans look to other places than the traditional news organizations for information. He contends that popular music, nonnews television and the film industry now serve to inform America's youth far more than newspapers or television news programs:

> Straight news—the Old News—is pooped, confused and broke. . . .
> In the place of the Old News, something dramatic is evolving, a new culture of information, a hybrid New News—dazzling, adolescent, irresponsible, fearless, frightening and powerful. The New News is a heady concoction, part Hollywood film and TV movie, part pop music and pop art, mixed with popular culture and celebrity magazines, tabloid telecasts, cable and home video.
> Increasingly, the New News is seizing the functions of mainstream journalism, sparking conversations and setting the country's social and political agenda. (p. 33)

Katz' contention that nontraditional forms of news are affecting American democracy is one that has merit. This is evidenced by the media's role in the 1992 presidential campaign: Larry King, MTV, and Arsenio Hall made as significant a contribution to the dialogue that surrounded the election as that made by the traditional news media. The "New News" media may also be serving to help contradict some of the myths about race that traditional journalistic conventions tend to support. As Katz (1992) writes, "Spike Lee is far ahead of his mainstream journalistic competitors on racial issues. So is [rapper] Ice Cube" (p. 35). Talk show discussions, feature films and some rap music videos have addressed issues related to race in a manner that arguably offers more perspective, more honesty. This is certainly an area worthy of more study.

Twenty-five years ago, the Kerner Commission assailed the news media for presenting a distorted picture of life for Americans of color. Though news organizations have made efforts— some sincere, some not—to change that picture, those efforts have not been entirely fruitful. America's racial myths—rooted in the nescience of hundreds of years of white supremacy—endure despite the best intentions of the news media. It may well be that the very nature of those media—and of the society in which they exist—may not allow them to function in a manner that will contribute to more accurate portrayals of life outside of the mainstream. That would require newsroom processes and social forces to be systematically questioned and altered. It would also require an awakening of mainstream American thought that would acknowledge the persistence of racism as a powerful force that has superseded true democracy in American society.

I am not optimistic about either of these possibilities. Newsrooms are not likely to change the established routines that dictate how events are covered. Despite journalism's trumpeted efforts as democracy's champion, when it comes to race the watchdog is snoozing comfortably in its doghouse. And a sudden American acknowledgment of its own prejudices and bigotry is not likely to come any time soon; political tokenism and economic lip service will continue to supplant any sincere advancement in the condition of America's poor and disenfranchised, especially those of color.

This study's contribution to media studies, then, is not in its identification of a problem that can be easily solved or eliminated. It is, rather, an attempt to identify both the blatant and the subtle ways in which race is mythologized in the news. Identification of the myths is only the beginning in understanding their consequences, their power. If there is reason to be optimistic, it is in the fact that cultural myths are not stagnant: They can change and evolve or be eliminated and forgotten. And the potent myth-making capacity of local television news could be turned on its head to refute the very myths it now sustains. That would be my hope for American journalism and American society— that the myths about race that they cling to will give way to a more accurate, more truthful perception of people of color that will make America more tolerant of its diversity and become a more equitable place for all of its peoples.

Appendix A
ALPHABETICAL LISTING OF TV MARKETS INCLUDED IN STUDY

City, State	(ADI*)	Station (Network)	Dates	Times = p.m.	Length
1. Atlanta, GA	(10)	WXIA (NBC)	1/18 + 19	6-7	2 hrs
2. Billings-Hardin, MT	(117)	KTVQ (CBS)	1/18 + 19	5:30-6	1 hr
3. Cheyenne, WY	(195)	KGWN (CBS)	1/18 + 19	5:30-6:30	2 hrs
4. Chicago, IL	(3)	WMAQ (NBC)	1/18 + 19	10-10:30	1 hr
5. Cincinnati, OH	(30)	WCPO (CBS)	1/18 + 19	5-6:30	3 hrs
6. Columbus, OH	(34)	WSYX (ABC)	1/18 @ 6-6:30	1/19 @ 10-10:30	1 hr
7. Dayton, OH	(53)	WHIO (CBS)	1/18 + 19	6-6:30	1 hr
8. Des Moines, IA	(70)	KCCI (CBS)	1/18 + 19	6-6:30	1 hr
9. Detroit, MI	(9)	WDIV (NBC)	1/18 + 19	11-11:30	1 hr
10. Fargo, ND	(108)	WDAY (ABC)	1/18 + 19	6-6:30	1 hr
11. Hattiesburg, MS	(164)	WDAM (NBC)	1/18 + 19	6-6:30	1 hr
12. Houston, TX	(11)	KTRK (ABC)	1/18 + 19	5-5:30	1 hr
13. Lafayette, LA	(119)	KLFY (CBS)	1/18 + 19	6-6:30	1 hr
14. Los Angeles, CA	(2)	KNBC (NBC)	1/18 + 19	6-6:30	1 hr
15. Milwaukee, WI	(28)	WITI (CBS)	1/18 + 19	6-6:30	1 hr
16. Minneapolis-St. Paul, MN	(13)	KARE (NBC)	1/18 + 19	6-6:30	1 hr
17. Nashville, TN	(33)	WTVF (CBS)	1/18 + 19	6-7	2 hrs
18. New Orleans, LA	(40)	WWL (CBS)	1/18 + 19	6-6:30	1 hr
19. New York, NY	(1)	WCBS (CBS)	1/18 + 19	6-6:30	1 hr
20. Norfolk-Portsmouth-Newport News, VA	(38)	WTKR (CBS)	1/18 + 19	6-6:30 1 hr	
21. Phoenix, AZ	(20)	KTVK (ABC)	1/18 + 19	6-6:30	1 hr
22. Portland, OR	(27)	KPTV (Ind.)	1/18 + 19	10-11	2 hrs
23. St. Louis, MO	(18)	KSDK (NBC)	1/18 + 19	5-5:30, 6-6:30	2 hrs

24. St. Petersburg, FL	(16)	WFLA (NBC)	1/18	6-6:30	1/2 hr
25. Salinas–Monterey, CA	(111)	KSBW (NBC)	1/18 + 19	6-7	2 hrs
26. Salt Lake City, UT	(42)	KSL (CBS)	1/19 + 20	6-7	2 hrs
27. San Francisco– Oakland–San Jose, CA	(5)	KPIX (CBS)	1/18 + 19	10-11	2 hrs
28. Seattle–Tacoma, WA	(14)	KOMO (ABC)	1/18	6-7	1 hr
29. Syracuse, NY	(66)	WTVH (CBS)	1/18 + 19	5:30-6:30	2 hrs

NOTE: * ADI = Area of Dominant Interest (market size) as listed by *Broadcasting and Cable Market Place 1992*.

Appendix B

RACE OF JOURNALISTS
WHO APPEARED ON CAMERA

	White	Black	Latino	Asian	Native American
Anchors 64 (*N*)	56 (88%)	7 (10%)	1 (2%)	0	0
Reporters: 238 (*N*)	201 (85%)	27 (11%)	8 (3%)	2 (1%)	0
Weather Casters: 34 (*N*)	31 (91%)	2 (6%)	1 (3%)	0	0
Sports Anchors and Reporters: 37 (*N*)	34 (92%)	2 (5%)	1 (3%)	0	0

Appendix C
TRANSCRIPT OF LAUREL, MS
KING PARADE/WDAM

Hattiesburg, MS WDAM/NBC
6 p.m./Jan. 18, 1993
King Parade: 27 seconds

(VIDEO = CAPS/audio = lower case)

CLOSE-UP OF ANCHOR BOB NOONAN

NOONAN: South Mississippians joined in today's national celebration of the Martin Luther King Holiday. The murdered civil rights
leader was honored in Laurel in this fifth avenue—er—fifth annual
parade . . .

LONG SHOT OF PARADE, LED BY HONOR GUARD. CUT TO FULL
SHOT OF FOUR GIRLS CARRYING BANNER WITH PICTURE OF MARTIN
LUTHER KING. CUT TO CLOSE-UP OF PICTURE.

NOONAN: . . . An honor guard carrying an American flag led about
75 participants from Sawmill Square Mall to the middle of downtown . . .

LONG SHOT OF ABOUT TEN CHILDREN ON BICYCLES WHO ARE PART OF PARADE

NOONAN: The parade was one of a series of Martin Luther King holiday events in Laurel that started over the weekend . . .

FULL SHOT OF FIVE CHILDREN CARRYING BANNER READING "SMART MOVES, THE BOYS AND GIRLS CLUB"

NOONAN: Organizers say they hope the commemoration will make young people more aware of his legacy and bring blacks as well as whites together.

Transcript reprinted with permission of WDAM-TV.

Appendix D
TRANSCRIPT OF
LEE TRIBUTE/WDAM

Hattiesburg, MS WDAM/NBC
6 p.m./Jan. 18, 1993
Lee Tribute: 60 seconds

CLOSE-UP OF ANCHOR WHITNEY VANN

VANN: While each of the fifty states honored the life and legacy of
Dr. Martin Luther King today, thousands of Southerners paid
tribute as well to Robert E. Lee . . .

MEDIUM SHOT OF PORTRAIT OF LEE. CUT TO FULL SHOT OF SIX
MEN IN CONFEDERATE UNIFORMS FIRING RIFLES INTO THE AIR.
CUT TO A CLOSE-UP OF THE BASE OF A STATUE WHICH READS, "TO
THE MEN AND WOMEN OF THE CONFEDERACY." CUT TO FULL SHOT
OF FIVE PEOPLE WATCHING. CUT TO FULL SHOT OF WOMAN IN
CIVIL WAR ERA-GARB PLACING A WREATH AT THE FOOT OF THE
STATUE. CUT TO FULL SHOT OF TOP OF STATUE, APPARENTLY LEE.

VANN: . . . For decades the birth date of the commander of the
Confederate forces has been commemorated throughout the South.

It's one of several special days including Confederate Memorial Day and Jefferson Davis' birthday observed nearly 130 years after the end of the Civil War. And a Hattiesburg member of the Sons of Confederate Veterans says Robert E. Lee is well deserving of the honor.

CUT TO FULL SHOT OF RICK FORTE ON A COUCH IN WHAT IS APPARENTLY HIS HOME. A CIVIL WAR UNIFORM AND OTHER APPARENT CONFEDERATE MEMORABILIA IS ON DISPLAY. (SHOT SHOWS FORTE'S T-SHIRT ON WHICH IS PRINTED A CONFEDERATE FLAG.) CUT TO MEDIUM SHOT OF UNIDENTIFIED REPORTER. CUT TO CLOSE-UP OF FORTE.

FORTE: He just stood for what a Southern gentleman stood for and what a soldier stood for—honor, you know, land, your home, honor, family. He stood for that.

VANN: Rick Forte is the man who discovered skeletal remains designated and reburied in 1979 as the official unknown Confederate soldier.

Transcript reprinted with permission of WDAM-TV.

Appendix E
TRANSCRIPT OF
SPEARFISHING/KARE

Minneapolis-St. Paul, MN KARE/NBC
6 p.m./Jan. 19, 1992
Spearfishing: 3:15

LONG SHOT OF SNOW-COVERED LAKE;
  MEDIUM SHOT OF A FISHERMAN SPEARING A FISH

PAUL MAGERS: A frozen blanket of ice covers the waters of Lake Mille
Lacs, but this serene setting is the centerpiece of Minnesota's hottest
controversy. The issue? Native American spearfishing.

  MEDIUM SHOT OF ANCHORS PAUL MAGERS AND PAT MILES ON
THE NEWS SET

MAGERS: . . . Today state officials and a Mille Lacs Band of Chippewa Indians reached a final agreement.

MILES: It sets the rules for spearing and netting on a part of the
lake, an agreement some anglers fiercely hate. KARE 11's Capitol
correspondent Dennis Stauffer has the details.

MEDIUM SHOT OF DENNIS STAUFFER STANDING IN THE ASSEM-
BLY ROOM OF THE STATE CAPITOL

STAUFFER: Paul, Pat, by finally making this agreement public, the
D.N.R. [Division of Natural Resources] has answered many of the
questions that have surrounded it. But that's showing no sign of
calming the controversy.

CLOSE-UP OF FISH BEING PULLED OUT OF AN ICE-FISHING HOLE
ON A LINE; SOUND ON TAPE AS FISHERMAN SAYS "THERE WE GO!
HO! HA!"; CLOSE-UP OF FISH ON ICE

STAUFFER: . . . Mille Lacs is Minnesota's premiere trophy fishing
lake, and under the agreement disclosed today, D.N.R. commissioner
Ron Sando says the lake will stay that way.

LONG SHOT OF SANDO SEATED AT THE HEAD TABLE OF A NEWS
CONFERENCE; HE IS SITTING NEXT TO A NATIVE AMERICAN REPRE-
SENTATIVE

SANDO: I think this agreement does protect the resources.

GRAPHIC OF MAP OF MILLE LACS LAKE; TREATY ZONE IS HIGH-
LIGHTED

STAUFFER: The agreement would create a six-thousand acre exclusive Indian treaty zone in the southwest corner of Lake Mille Lacs next
to the Mille Lacs' band reservation, plus another six nonexclusive
sites around the state.

GRAPHIC OUTLINES TERMS OF AGREEMENT: "NETTING AND SPEAR-
ING ALLOWED/HARVEST APPORTIONED ACCORDING TO LIMIT ON
ENTIRE LAKE/$10 MILLION PAYMENT TO TRIBE/CEDE 7,500 ACRES
OF LAND"

STAUFFER: . . . Netting and spearing of fish would be allowed, as
long as it's done for subsistence, not commercial purposes. And the
allowable Indian harvest on Lake Mille Lacs would be apportioned
according to the overall limit for the lake. The agreement also calls
for the state to pay the tribe 10 million dollars over the next 4½
years and cede 7,500 acres of state-owned land to the tribe.

SEVERAL LONG SHOTS OF NEWS CONFERENCE; CLOSE-UP OF SANDO

STAUFFER: . . . Sando says the alternative is for the state to risk losing a law suit filed by Native Americans.

SANDO: We could possibly lose as much as half the fish in Mille Lacs Lake and if that were the case I think it would have a tremendous impact on sport fishing, tourism and local economy.

LONG SHOT OF FISH BEING SPEARED AT NIGHT FROM A BOAT; CLOSE-UP OF FISH ON SPEAR

STAUFFER: Sando points to a similar lawsuit which Wisconsin tribes won, granting them 50% of the fish in that area.

GRAPHIC OF MAP OF THE STATE OF MINNESOTA WITH 1837 TREATY AREA (INCLUDING MILLE LACS LAKE) HIGHLIGHTED

STAUFFER: . . . The same 1837 treaty covered the same area in western Minnesota.

LONG SHOT OF GROUP OF ABOUT 75 MEN ON CAPITOL STEPS; SOME HOLD SIGNS; CLOSE-UP OF ONE SIGN READS "NO NETS"; ANOTHER READS "GOVERNOR CARLSON—WE NEED YOUR HELP"

STAUFFER: . . . But critics, which include sports and tourist groups, say that Indians gave up their rights long ago under subsequent treaties and that Minnesota would win in court.

CLOSE-UP OF BUD GRANT

GRANT: I don't think it's got to be a deal.

LONG, LOW ANGLE SHOT OF GRANT; HE IS SITTING IN FRONT OF A WALL FULL OF MINNESOTA VIKINGS FOOTBALL MEMORABILIA, INCLUDING FRAN TARKENTON'S NUMBER 10 JERSEY

STAUFFER: Bud Grant is the honorary chairman of the Save Mille Lacs Association.

CLOSE-UP OF GRANT

GRANT: I think there is a right and a wrong. Why should one group of people be allowed to do something another group of people cannot do? Why should they have exclusive rights?

MEDIUM SHOT OF STAUFFER IN THE ASSEMBLY ROOM AT THE CAPITOL

STAUFFER: . . . Paul, Pat, they've gotten to this point now, but they still have to win approval from the tribe and from lawmakers, and getting support here is going to be a challenge. So far, a number of lawmakers have come forward to criticize this pact, and no one has yet come forward to sponsor the bill, which is necessary to even bring it up for debate.

LONG SHOT OF BACK OF ANCHORS ON SET LOOKING AT STAUFFER ON A LARGE MONITOR; REVERSE SHOT OF THE TWO ANCHORS LOOKING AT THE MONITOR

MAGERS: Dennis, is the tribe happy with it as well?

SAME SHOT OF STAUFFER AT CAPITOL

STAUFFER: Well, their negotiator, which is their sort of commissioner of the division of natural resources, if you please, was at the news conference today. He supports it. He helped negotiate it. They still have to draft their own regulations, which they say will be consistent with state regulations and handled responsibly, but then they're going to have a referendum, and the outcome of that is not certain, although it's much more likely to be positive it appears right now than here in the legislature.

MEDIUM SHOT OF TWO ANCHORS LOOKING AT MONITOR

MILES: And this has the potential, does it not Dennis, to become probably the most controversial issue before the state legislature this year?

SAME SHOT OF STAUFFER

STAUFFER: It certainly has the potential to generate the most sparks around here. Yes.

Transcript reprinted with permission of KARE-TV.

Appendix F
TRANSCRIPT OF NEW ORLEANS
KING DAY COVERAGE/WWL

New Orleans, LA WWL/CBS
6 p.m./January 18, 1993
King Day Coverage: 4:04

LONG SHOT OF COANCHORS ANGELA HILL AND JOHN SNELL ON
NEWS SET

HILL: New Orleanians joined the nation today in paying respect to
slain civil rights leader Dr. Martin Luther King, Jr.

SNELL: A week of events culminated this afternoon in a march and
rally. We have two reports beginning with Susan Roberts.

FULL SHOT OF MAN IN RELIGIOUS COLLAR MARCHING AND
CARRYING A SIGN; GRAPHIC READS "CELEBRATING A DREAM"; MAN
SAYS TO CAMERA, "THE DREAM LIVES ON AND ON"; SEVERAL LONG
SHOTS OF MARCHERS

ROBERTS: The parade was only a start of what was an event to
some but a painful day of remembrance for others. Dr. Martin Luther

King died fighting for what he believed in. This man won't let it be forgotten.

CLOSE-UP OF UNIDENTIFIED MAN

UNIDENTIFIED MAN: We had a man who was very dedicated to some very serious principles that we need to live by in order to get along, because as we see, you know, a lot of people are not getting along the way they're supposed to.

LONG SHOT OF MARCHERS

ROBERTS: King's day is a time for a celebration in part in that we can take pride in the progress, but look forward to even more unity.

CLOSE-UP OF SECOND UNIDENTIFIED MAN

SECOND UNIDENTIFIED MAN: He has made some contributions to society for all people, not just for black people but for people of all races.

CLOSE-UP OF THIRD UNIDENTIFIED MAN

THIRD UNIDENTIFIED MAN: Every year it's growing and I think it's a real positive expression of people remembering Martin Luther King. I like the numbers of people, the different variety of people that came out. I think it's a great celebration.

LONG SHOT OF MAN SINGING ON STAGE; MEDIUM SHOT OF UNIDENTIFIED SPEAKER; SOUND ON TAPE IS BRIEFLY HEARD, THEN MEDIUM SHOT OF ROBERTS

ROBERTS: The day's activities ended at a rally in Armstrong Park. Various speakers took to the stage urging everyone to keep hope alive. The celebration is now over but the work is not. Organizers say it is up to people of all races to keep Dr. King's message alive, not just on this day but all year long. Susan Roberts, Channel 4, Eyewitness News.

BLACK AND WHITE FILM OF KING LEADING A MARCH; GRAPHIC READS "CARRYING THE MESSAGE"; VIDEOTAPE OF NEW ORLEANS KING DAY MARCH—LONG SHOT OF MARCHERS

RENSHAW: I'm Elizabeth Renshaw. Martin Luther King, Jr., led the charge for civil rights in this country, and some who joined him are still carrying that message today.

FULL SHOT OF SIMMIE HARVIE MARCHING; LONG SHOT OF CHURCH

RENSHAW: The Reverend Simmie Harvie was one of those who joined King, even before many knew about his cause. King met him and others at this uptown church, where they founded the Southern Christian Leadership Conference.

CLOSE-UP OF HARVIE

HARVIE: He had what is called a magnet. You meet him, you walk with him, he had a drawing power.

MEDIUM SHOT OF RENSHAW WITH MORRIS JEFF, SR.

RENSHAW: Morris Jeff, Sr., says you can still hear King's voice echoing today.

CLOSE-UP OF JEFF; GRAPHIC IDENTIFIES HIM AS "CIVIL RIGHTS LEADER"

JEFF: He was soft-spoken, but what he said had meaning.

BLACK AND WHITE FILM—LONG SHOT OF KING DELIVERING "I HAVE A DREAM SPEECH"; WE HEAR PART OF SPEECH: "I HAVE A DREAM THAT MY FOUR LITTLE CHILDREN WILL ONE DAY LIVE IN A NATION WHERE THEY WILL NOT BE JUDGED BY THE COLOR OF THEIR SKIN BUT BY THE CONTENT OF THEIR CHARACTER. I HAVE A DREAM TODAY."

BLACK AND WHITE FILM OF CIVIL RIGHTS MARCH; WHITE DEMONSTRATORS TAUNT MARCHERS; ONE WHITE MAN HOLDS A CONFEDERATE BATTLE FLAG

RENSHAW: But that soft-spoken voice soon reached millions, and many hated his words of peace.

HARVIE: They were rough on us. When we would break up a meeting, we had to get off the street simply because people would be laying for you. They'd beat you up.

RENSHAW: Even King seemed to sense the danger.

CLOSE-UP OF KING DELIVERING SPEECH: "LONGEVITY HAS ITS PLACE, BUT I'M NOT CONCERNED ABOUT THAT NOW. I JUST WANT TO DO GOD'S WILL."

CLOSE-UP OF HARVIE

HARVIE: A brother would always tell me, "You're going to get killed following that man." We could have gotten killed with King, but we didn't care. Our lives were with him.

CLOSE-UP OF LORRAINE MOTEL SIGN; LONG SHOT OF BALCONY WHERE KING WAS SHOT; MEDIUM SHOT OF KING IN HIS CASKET; LONG SHOT OF NEW ORLEANS MARCH

RENSHAW: But King didn't stay with them long. An assassin's bullet silenced his speech, but followers say it did not silence his message. Elizabeth Renshaw, Eyewitness News.

MEDIUM SHOT OF ANCHOR JOHN SNELL; GRAPHIC LISTS TIMES OF EVENING'S EVENTS

SNELL: There are a couple more Martin Luther King, Jr., events tonight. The Versailles Arms community in New Orleans East hosts a ceremony and parade beginning at 6:30 tonight, and nationally known TV producer and journalist Tony Brown addresses a banquet at the Four Columns at 7:00.

Transcript reprinted with permission of WWL-TV.

Appendix G
TRANSCRIPT OF PHOENIX, AZ
KING DAY COVERAGE/KTVK

Phoenix, AZ KTVK/ABC
6 p.m./January 18, 1993
King Day Coverage: 1:05

MEDIUM SHOT OF COANCHOR PATTI KIRKPATRICK NEXT TO
"KING DAY" GRAPHIC

KIRKPATRICK: Well, the rain did stay away just long enough this
morning to allow the Martin Luther King March to go on as planned.

LONG SHOT OF LARGE GROUP OF MARCHERS ON STREET; SOUND
ON TAPE IS HEARD AS MARCHERS CHANT IN RESPONSE TO LEADER:
"WE FINALLY GOT IT/KING DAY/WAS IT WORTH IT? /YES."

KIRKPATRICK: An estimated 10,000 people marched through downtown Phoenix today to commemorate the birthday of the slain civil
rights leader.

SEVERAL SHOTS OF MARCHERS

KIRKPATRICK: . . . This was truly a victory march since voters approved the statewide holiday just last November. The march ended with a rally at Wesley Bolin Plaza.

MEDIUM SHOT OF RABBI ROBERT KRAVITZ

KRAVITZ: What was a landmark for the state of Arizona is now a benchmark for the rest of the country. We voted for the holiday, and we passed it.

MEDIUM SHOT OF THE REVEREND WARREN STEWART

STEWART: It's something they should have done years ago. So it's mixed emotions: Yes, there's joy, but—hey—it's about time.

SEVERAL LONG SHOTS OF PARADE IN MESA, AZ

KIRKPATRICK: Now this is not a paid city holiday parade in Mesa, but many residents celebrated by holding a march for unity. The parade made its way through the downtown streets. The theme of this first community-wide King Day effort is a celebration of diversity. Participants say they want people to know that King Day is not only a holiday for minorities.

Transcript reprinted with permission of KTVK-TV.

Appendix H
TRANSCRIPT OF BILLINGS, MT
KING DAY COVERAGE/KTVQ

Billings, MT KTVQ/CBS
5:30 p.m./January 18, 1993
King Day Coverage: 4:12

MEDIUM SHOT OF ANCHOR GUS KOERNIG

KOERNIG: For the first time, Americans all across the country are
celebrating Martin Luther King Day. Good evening, I'm Gus Koernig.
It's hard to believe anyone might not have heard of Dr. Martin
Luther King, Jr. The civil rights leader was shot to death in 1968,
and today the nation commemorates his birth. In Billings a procession and a church service will mark the occasion. The ceremony
begins at seven at American Lutheran Church, and that's where the
News Station's Jennifer Elliot is right now. Jennifer?

SPLIT SCREEN WITH MEDIUM SHOTS OF KOERNIG AND ELLIOT,
THEN JUST ELLIOT

ELLIOT: Gus, it's not a bad night for a procession out here. It begins
at American Lutheran, where I am right now. It starts at 7 o'clock,

and it's a flashlight procession which will curve all throughout downtown Billings and end up at First Methodist, where a Martin Luther King Christian unity service will be held. Now with me is Greg Krueger, who is with the Billings Ecumenical Council, and he's going to answer a few questions about the parade tonight. Tell me a little bit about the route it goes on.

FULL SHOT OF ELLIOT AND KRUEGER; CLOSE-UP OF KRUEGER

KRUEGER: Well, we start—as you said—right here at American Lutheran, and we'll go from here over to First Baptist Church, and then down the street to St. Luke's Episcopal Church, kind of around the corner to St. Patrick's Catholic Church and down the block a little ways, and we'll end up at First Methodist.

ELLIOT: And that service starts at 7:30, correct?

KRUEGER: That starts at 7:30, yeah, depending on how slowly we walk.

ELLIOT: Now what about if people are a little late at 7? Can they meet up along the way?

KRUEGER: Sure. A lot of different people will be joining us from the different churches as we go along. Not everybody is going to start right here.

ELLIOT: This is the ninth year of the Christian unity service, but it was never specifically to celebrate Martin Luther King's birthday. Why is that different this year?

KRUEGER: Well, we decided that with the rise of some different hate groups—not only worldwide but here in Billings, too—that we would join with the Montana Association of Churches and the Wayman Chapel and show our support for Martin Luther King's holiday and his message of social justice and peace and tolerance. It's the first time we've done that, and I think it's a good move.

ELLIOT: This is the first year with Wayman Chapel, too, right?

KRUEGER: Yes, it is the first year with Wayman Chapel, and we're looking forward to it. Their choir is going to be performing at the service. It's going to be very nice.

FULL SHOT OF ELLIOT AND KRUEGER

ELLIOT: Do you see racism as a bigger problem—seeing the growth of hate groups and all that here in Billings—do you see that as a bigger problem and is that part of the reason why the service is being celebrated the way it is?

KRUEGER: It is a big problem anywhere. Even if there are just a few people involved, it makes it a big problem because it is such a divisive type of thing. The Wayman Chapel has shown some concern over that and we wanted to show our support with them. Coretta Scott King said—just last night I think it was—there is a resurgence of hate in our society as well as the world society and we want to show our support for people with tolerance.

ELLIOT: What is the sermon going to be about tonight?

KRUEGER: Rev. Dr. Kinnamon will be giving a sermon on racism in churches, and he's kind of an authority. He's from the Lexington Seminary in Lexington, Kentucky—Theological Seminary. He is an excellent speaker. He is nationally and world known, and his topic will be racism and tolerance basically.

ELLIOT: Okay, thank you very much Greg Krueger. This will begin at 7 o'clock at American Lutheran. You can march your way over to First Methodist, where the service will begin at 7:30. In Billings, I'm Jennifer Elliot reporting live for the news station.

MEDIUM SHOT OF KOERNIG NEXT TO "KING HOLIDAY" GRAPHIC

KOERNIG: Thanks Jennifer. Martin Luther King's dream included *all* Americans, and the campaign for equal rights for Native Americans had its beginnings around the time Dr. King was assassinated nearly 25 years ago. Native American leaders in our area say change has been slow in coming, and there is still a lot of progress to be made.

CLOSE-UP OF ALDA SMALL; GRAPHIC READS "INTERTRIBAL RE-SOURCE CENTER"

SMALL: If we can just build a basic understanding of one another's culture—traditions, lifestyles, family systems—I definitely believe that some of these problems with racism can be alleviated.

MEDIUM SHOT OF KOERNIG

KOERNIG: Small says one way to build that understanding is providing greater ethnic representation in local and national government. She hopes the new administrations in Helena and Washington will pay more attention to needs of all ethnic and racial
minorities.

Transcript reprinted with permission of KTVQ-TV.

References

Abrams, M. H. (1988). *A glossary of literary terms*. Fort Worth: Harcourt Brace Jovanovich.

American Society of Newspaper Editors (ASNE). (1992). *Minority employment survey*. Washington, DC: Author.

Bagdikian, B. (1983). *The media monopoly*. Boston: Beacon.

Barthes, R. (1972). *Mythologies* (Jonathan Cape Ltd., Trans.). New York: Hill & Wang. (Original work published 1957)

Bell, K. (1993, January 19). March: Memories, music honor King. *The Times-Picayune*, pp. A1, A6.

Bird, S. E., & Dardenne, R. W. (1988). Myth, chronicle, and story: Exploring the narrative qualities of news. In J. W. Carey (Ed.), *Media, myths, and narratives: Television and the press* (pp. 67-86). Newbury Park, CA: Sage.

Bobo, L. (1988). Group conflict, prejudice, and the paradox of contemporary racial attitudes. In P. A. Katz & D. A. Taylor (Eds.), *Eliminating racism* (pp. 85-114). New York: Plenum.

Boskin, J. (1980). Denials: The media view of dark skins and the city. In B. Rubin (Ed.), *Small voices and great trumpets: Minorities and the media* (pp. 141-147). New York: Praeger.

Breed, W. (1960). Social control in the newsroom: A functional analysis. In W. Schramm (Ed.), *Mass communications* (pp. 178-197). Urbana: University of Illinois Press.

Broadcasting & cable marketplace. (1992). New Providence, NJ: R. R. Bower.

Campbell, J. (1988). *The power of myth.* Garden City, NY: Doubleday.

Campbell, R. (1991a). *60 Minutes and the news: A mythology for Middle America.* Urbana: University of Illinois Press.

Campbell, R. (1991b). Word vs. image: Elitism, popularity and TV news. *Television Quarterly, 26*(1), 73-81.

Carey, J. W. (1989). *Communication as culture: Essays on media and society.* Winchester, MA: Unwin Hyman.

Cohen, S., & Young, J. (1973). *The manufacture of news: A reader.* Beverly Hills, CA: Sage.

Dates, J. L., & Barlow, W. (1990). *Split image: African Americans in the mass media.* Washington, DC: Howard University Press.

Dellios, H. (1993, January 18). How national press sizes it up: Joy over holiday has wary edge. *The Phoenix Gazette,* p. A2.

Dimmick, J. (1974). The gatekeeper: An uncertain theory. *Journalism Monographs, 37.*

Ehli, N. (1993, January 19). March honors King's beliefs. *The Billings Gazette,* p. B1.

Entman, R. M. (1990). Modern racism and the images of blacks in local television news. *Critical Studies in Mass Communication, 7*(4), 332-345.

Entman, R. M. (1992). Blacks in the news: Television, modern racism and cultural change. *Journalism Quarterly, 69*(2), 341-361.

Epstein, E. J. (1973). *News from nowhere.* New York: Random House.

Essed, P. (1991). *Understanding everyday racism.* Newbury Park, CA: Sage.

Fiske, J., & Hartley, J. (1978). *Reading television.* London: Methuen.

Freeman, G. (1991). Lamenting our lettuce-heavy newsroom salad. *Quill, 79*(4), 3-5.

Gaertner, S. L., & Dovidio, J. F. (1986). *Prejudice, discrimination, and racism.* Orlando: Academic Press.

Gans, H. (1979). *Deciding what's news.* New York: Pantheon.

Geertz, C. (1983). Common sense as a cultural system. In *Local knowledge: Further essays in interpretive anthropology.* New York: Basic Books.

Gist, M. E. (1990). Minorities in media imagery. *Newspaper Research Journal, 11*(3), 52-63.

Gray, H. (1986). Television and the new black man: Black male images in prime-time situation comedy. *Media, Culture and Society, 8,* 223-242.

Gray, H. (1991). Television, black Americans, and the American dream. In R. K. Avery & D. Eason (Eds.), *Critical perspectives on media and society* (pp. 294-305). New York: Guilford.

Hacker, A. (1992). *Two nations: Black and white, separate, hostile, and unequal*. New York: Scribner.

Hall, S. (1973a). The determinations of news photographs. In S. Cohen & J. Young (Eds.), *The manufacture of news* (pp. 176-190). Beverly Hills, CA: Sage.

Hall, S. (1973b). A world at one with itself. In S. Cohen & J. Young (Eds.), *The manufacture of news* (pp. 85-94). Beverly Hills, CA: Sage.

Hall, S. (1980). Encoding/decoding. In S. Hall, D. Hobson, A. Lowe, & P. Wills (Eds.), *Culture, media, language* (pp. 128-138). London: Hutchinson.

Hambrick, G. (1993, January 19). King's quest filled with "love, logic." *The Columbus Dispatch*, p. A1.

Hartley, J. (1984). Out of bounds: The myth of marginality. In L. Masterman (Ed.), *Television mythologies: Stars, shows and signs* (pp. 118-127). London: Comedia Publishing Group.

Himmelstein, H. (1984). *TV myth and the American mind*. New York: Praeger.

hooks, b. (1992). *Black looks: Race and representation*. Boston: South End.

Jhally, S., & Lewis, J. (1992). *Enlightened racism: The Cosby Show, audiences, and the myth of the American dream*. Boulder: Westview.

Johnson, B., & Bullard-Johnson, M. (1988). *Who's what and where: A directory and reference book on America's minority journalists*. Columbia, MO: Who's What and Where Publishing.

Johnson, P. B., & Sears, D. O. (1971). Black invisibility, the press, and the Los Angeles riot. *American Journal of Sociology, 76*(1), 698-721.

Katz, J. (1992, March 5). Rock, rap and movies bring you the news. *Rolling Stone*, pp. 33-35, 40, 78.

Kerner Commission. (1968). *Report of the National Advisory Commission on Civil Disorders*. New York: E. P. Dutton.

Kotz, N. (1979). The minority struggle for a place in the newsroom. *Columbia Journalism Review, 17*(6), 23-31.

Kurtz, H. (1994). *Media circus: The trouble with America's newspapers*. New York: Random House.

Lazarsfeld, P. F., & Merton, R. K. (1960). Mass communication, popular taste and organized social action. In W. Schramm (Ed.), *Mass communications* (pp. 492-512). Urbana: University of Illinois Press.

Lentz, R. (1991). The search for strategic silence: Discovering what journalism leaves out. *American Journalism*, *8*(1), 10-26.

Lévi-Strauss, C. (1967). The structural study of myth. In *Structural anthropology* (C. Jacobson & B. Grundfest Schoef, Trans.). Garden City, NY: Anchor-Doubleday.

Lichter, S. R., Rothman, S., & Lichter, L. S. (1986). *The media elite*. Bethesda: Adler & Adler.

Lippmann, W. (1922). *Public opinion*. New York: Macmillan.

Lyle, J., & Wilcox, W. (1963). Television news—An interim report. *Journal of Broadcasting*, *7*(2), 157-166.

MacDonald, J. F. (1983). *Blacks and white TV: Afro-Americans in television since 1948*. Chicago: Nelson-Hall.

MacNeil, R. (1968). *The people machine*. New York: Harper & Row.

Mannes, E. (Producer & Director). (1993, April 27). L.A. is burning— Five reports from a divided city. *Frontline* (Show #1117, PBS). Los Angeles: Elena Mannes Productions.

Martindale, C. (1986). *The white press in black America*. Westport, CT: Greenwood Press.

Martindale, C. (1990a). Changes in newspaper images of black Americans. *Newspaper Research Journal*, *11*(1), 40-50.

Martindale, C. (1990b). Coverage of black Americans in four major newspapers, 1950-1989. *Newspaper Research Journal*, *11*(3), 96-112.

McCloy, M. (1993, January 19). Lawmaker: Arizona hurt by racism. *The Phoenix Gazette*, p. B1.

McConahay, J. B. (1982). Self-interest versus racial attitudes as correlates of anti-busing attitudes in Louisville: Is it the buses or the blacks? *Journal of Politics*, *44*, 692-720.

McConahay, J. B. (1986). Modern racism, ambivalence, and the modern racism scale. In S. L. Gaertner & J. F. Dovidio (Eds.), *Prejudice, discrimination, and racism* (pp. 91-125). Orlando: Academic Press.

Milton S. Eisenhower Foundation. (1993). *Investing in children and our youth, reconstructing our cities: Doing what works to reverse the betrayal of American democracy, in commemoration of the twenty-fifth anniversary of the National Advisory Commission on Civil Disorders* (Prepublication copy). Washington, DC: Author.

Mixon, W. (1989). New southern mythology. In C. R. Wilson & W. Ferris (Eds.), *Encyclopedia of Southern culture* (pp. 1113-1115). Chapel Hill: University of North Carolina Press.

Moore, L. W. (1990). How your news looks to us. *Columbia Journalism Review, 28*(4), 21-24.

Nelson, J. (1993). *Volunteer slavery: My authentic Negro experience.* Chicago: Noble Press.

Okantah, M. S. (1993). America's poem, or, 81 seconds and 56 blows. In H. R. Madhubuti (Ed.), *Why LA happened* (pp. 136-140). Chicago: Third World Press.

Parks, R. (1940). News as a form of knowledge: A chapter in the sociology of knowledge. *The American Journal of Sociology, 45*(5), 669-686.

Pauly, J. J. (1991). A beginner's guide to doing qualitative research in mass communications. *Journalism Monographs, 125.*

Pease, E. C. (1989). Kerner plus 20: Minority news coverage in the Columbus Dispatch. *Newspaper Research Journal, 10*(3), 17-38.

Pinckney, A. (1993). Rodney King and Dred Scott. In H. R. Madhubuti (Ed.), *Why LA happened* (pp. 41-48). Chicago: Third World Press.

Powers, R. (1977). *The newscasters.* New York: St. Martin's.

Rashad, A. (1988). *Rashad: Vikes, mikes, and something on the backside.* New York: Viking.

Raum, T. (1993, January 19). Clinton ready for nation's mountaintop: Honors King on hectic day. *The Times-Picayune,* pp. A1, A5.

Reed, I. (1991, April 9). Tuning out network bias. *The New York Times,* p. A25.

Reilly, J. (1993a, January 18). King's legacy: A changed world. *Syracuse Herald-Journal,* p. B1.

Reilly, J. (1993b, January 19). Classmate echoes King's message. *Syracuse Herald-Journal,* p. B1.

Riede, P. (1993, January 18). Reality defers King's dream. *The Post-Standard,* p. A1.

Roper Organization. (1982). *Trends in attitudes toward television and other media: A twenty-four year review.* New York: Author.

Roper Organization. (1993). *America's watching: Public attitudes toward television.* New York: Network Television Association.

Rubin, B. (Ed.). (1980). *Small voices and great trumpets: Minorities and the media.* New York: Praeger.

Schudson, M. (1978). *Discovering the news.* New York: Basic Books.

Schultz, E. (1988, January). Toward the challenge of change. *RTDNA Communicator,* p. 91.

Sears, D. O. (1988). Symbolic racism. In P. A. Katz & D. A. Taylor (Eds.), *Eliminating racism* (pp. 53-84). New York: Plenum.

Seiter, E. (1987). Semiotics in television. In R. C. Allen (Ed.), *Channels of discourse* (pp. 17-41). Chapel Hill: University of North Carolina Press.

Sharp, S. A. (1989). Mythic South: Family. In C. R. Wilson & W. Ferris (Eds.), *Encyclopedia of Southern culture* (pp. 1104-1105). Chapel Hill: University of North Carolina Press.

Siebert, F. S., Peterson, T., & Schramm, W. (1956). *Four theories of the press: The authoritarian, libertarian, social responsibility and communist concepts of what the press should be and do.* Urbana: University of Illinois Press.

Simmons, C. E. (1993). The Los Angeles rebellion: Class, race and misinformation. In H. R. Madhubuti (Ed.), *Why LA happened* (pp. 141-155). Chicago: Third World Press.

Smokes, S. (1993, January 18). A challenge for whites to consider. *The Post Standard*, p. E1.

Stein, M. L. (1992). Concerned about diversity. *Editor and Publisher, 125*(19), 23, 40.

Stone, V. A. (1988a). Pipelines and dead ends: Jobs held by minorities and women in broadcast news. *Mass Comm Review, 15*(2 & 3), 10-19.

Stone, V. A. (1988b). Trends in the status of minorities and women in broadcast news. *Journalism Quarterly, 65*(2), 288-293.

Thornburn, D. (1987). Television as an aesthetic medium. *Critical Studies in Mass Communication, 4*(2), 161-173.

Trimble, J. E. (1988). Stereotypical images, American Indians, and prejudice. In P. A. Katz & D. A. Taylor (Eds.), *Eliminating racism* (pp. 181-202). New York: Plenum.

Tuchman, G. (1978). *Making news: A study in the construction of reality.* New York: Free Press.

Tucker, C. (1994, January 18). Dream in danger. *The Times-Picayune*, p. B5.

U.S. Commission on Civil Rights. (1977). *Window dressing on the set: Women and minorities in television.* Washington, DC: Government Printing Office.

U.S. Department of Commerce. (1990). *1990 census of population and housing.* Washington, DC: Author.

Van Dijk, T. A. (1988a). How "they" hit the headlines: Ethnic minorities and the press. In G. Smitherman Donaldson & T. A. van Dijk (Eds.), *Discourse and discrimination* (pp. 128-138). Detroit: Wayne State University Press.

Van Dijk, T. A. (1988b). *News analysis: Case studies of international and national news in the press*. Hillsdale, NJ: Lawrence Erlbaum.

Van Dijk, T. A. (1988c). *News as discourse*. Hillsdale, NJ: Lawrence Erlbaum.

Watts, R. (1993, January 19). King's daughter chides Clinton. *The Times-Picayune*, p. A2.

Weaver, P. (1981). Newspaper news and television news. In R. Adler (Ed.), *Understanding television: Essays on television as a social and cultural force* (pp. 277-294). New York: Praeger.

West, C. (1993). *Race matters*. Boston: Beacon.

Wilson, C. C., II, & Gutiérrez, F. (1985). *Minorities and media: Diversity and the end of mass communication*. Beverly Hills, CA: Sage.

Wilson, W. J. (1987). *The truly disadvantaged: The inner city, the underclass, and public policy*. Chicago: University of Chicago Press.

Index

About the Author

Christopher P. Campbell is Assistant Professor in the Department of Communication at Xavier University in New Orleans, where he teaches courses in journalism, mass communication and media criticism. He holds a Ph.D. in communication from the University of Southern Mississippi, where he received fellowships from the National Endowment for the Humanities and from the United Negro College Fund's Charles A. Dana Faculty Improvement Fund. He earned an M.S. in Mass Communication at the University of Southern Illinois at Edwardsville and a B.A. in English at Webster College in St. Louis. Before beginning his graduate studies, he taught high school English and journalism for 8 years in St. Louis. While working on his master's degree, he worked as a newspaper reporter and completed an internship as an assignment editor at a St. Louis television station.